I0450206

DREAM

DREAM

Andre Morissette

Authors Choice Press
San Jose New York Lincoln Shanghai

Dream

All Rights Reserved © 2000 by Mr. Andre Morissette

No part of this book may be reproduced or transmitted in any form or by any means, graphic, electronic, or mechanical, including photocopying, recording, taping, or by any information storage or retrieval system, without the permission in writing from the publisher.

Authors Choice Press
an imprint of iUniverse.com, Inc.

For information address:
iUniverse.com, Inc.
5220 S 16th, Ste. 200
Lincoln, NE 68512
www.iuniverse.com

ISBN: 0-595-14343-1

Printed in the United States of America

CONTENTS

First Chapter   3

Second Chapter   11

Third Chapter   22

Fourth Chapter   33

Fifth Chapter   46

Sixth Chapter   63

Seventh Chapter   73

Eighth Chapter   88

Ninth Chapter   98

Tenth Chapter   111

Eleventh Chapter   131

Dream

Twelfth chapter   *144*

Thirteenth Chapter   *158*

Fourteenth Chapter   *171*

Fifteenth Chapter   *186*

Sixteenth Chapter   *198*

DREAM

First Chapter

As one approaches fifty and feels that life has passed you by, the impression that it is too late to start over is quite imminent.

When one has lived in a world overflowing with great activity such as a government position and then finds himself in the country with sole companions being the wind, rain and snow, eventually, the feeling of uselessness becomes unbearable and life unbelievably depressing.

However, for John Chabot, this could have been a blessing should it had remained just as such. But, finding himself secluded at the very end of a dirt road leading away from a small unknown village in Quebec, in an infectious and unhealthy home, distraught and constantly remembering his past as though a new reality could immerge from it, he appeared having the weight of all the world's misery, sadness and remorse upon his shoulders.

In Ste-Cecile, people spend the majority of their time working the land and therefore only have the opportunity to meet and gossip during Sunday mass. Whether it is religious devotions or a social excuse, this is the perfect occasion for the village loud mouths to spread their weekly rumors. Obviously, there is not only land being cultivated in Ste-Cecile.

It is always the same people who begin this play; Rosilda the widow, Eugenia the postmaster, Gerard the vegetable merchant and Alphonse who is an old retired farmer. The subjects are as numerous as there are followers in the church and one can hear whispering as the next victim of these rumors passes by.

Dressed in an extremely battered coat, complimented by worned shoes covered in dirt, fallowed with his traditional three day beard, his wrinkles covering his face like an autumn field having been ploughed, and with swollen eyes John leaves the church staring at the ground in an attempt to avoid noticing anyone who may be staring or searching for a chance meeting.

With a lack of delicacy or due to awkwardness, the locals turn their backs to John giving him room to pass. As he approaches the conversations dull down and no sooner has he passed that they retake on a regular note.

- *He could at least wash himself; whispers one woman to another.*
  What disgusting smell; replies the other.
- *Having been so influential within the government and having fallen so low; exclaims a man.*
- *Yeah…all of it because of the damn alcohol; continues another.*

Acting as though he had not heard a word of this, John heads towards his aged and tired mare, which is quite a contrast with all the automobiles parked in front of the church.

He painfully climbs on board his rusted buggy and discretely gives his horse the order to advance.

The citizens standing on the church porch follow him with their eyes and continue their discussions. Some of them feel pity for John; others just don't trust him whereas the majorities feel repugnance that they just cannot hide but absolutely nobody feels indifference when it comes to John Chabot.

On Main Street, some children are hiding behind the bushes just waiting for John to pass them by.

- *I swear that he's evil, my mother told me so. She said I'd best keep my distance because he catches children and sells them to the devil.*
- *Of course not, replies another, my dad says that he's only a bad drunk, who killed his wife.*
- *People say that every night you can see lightening coming from his house and if you try to approach it, huge dogs will tear you apart, replied a third child*

While passing these children, John weekly salutes them, hoping to calm their fears of him. But, realizing John had noticed them, the children flee in fear and cry out for help.

Feeling quite uncomfortable about this, John commands his horse to pick up the pace and disappears further down the road.

As usual, he anxiously heads down the fourth road leading to his home while dusting himself off every time a vehicle passes which leaves him covered in dirt.

An all terrain truck passes him at which point one of the four young boys taking place on board yells to him:

- *Hey Johnny, how about one for the road; and being encouraged by the laughter of his friends, holds a beer out in John's direction.*

John lowers his eyes and angrily mumbles a few words to himself.

In approach of the area on the fourth road where houses and barns leave way to dense forests, John continues his way even further to finally reach his haven.

Upon arrival, he leads his horse to the stable, feeds her a modest portion of grain and hay to then regain his own quarters.

John opens his rustic and squeaking door with his foot. It is notice-able that there is no lock or chain installed on this door. Found before him is a single, dark and colorless room. The kitchen, his bedroom, the living room…it's three rooms in one.

A small area found in the corner and separated only by curtains gives way to a bathroom. This room is composed of a filthy toilet, a single sink covered in unused portions of soap and traces of oil, and a bath where a dark brown ring marks the level of water one can maybe find in it at some occasion.

John mechanically heads towards the cupboards above the kitchen sink and takes out a half-empty bottle. His most loyal companion; PIERRE. He talks to it as if it were an old friend and confidant.

Pierre is the name of his liquor. He addresses it as Pierre Smirnoff.

John only feeds himself with liquor and cigarettes.

He finally sits himself in a couch that blends in very well with the rest of his decor. Very dusty, torn and covered with debris. Sitting comfort-ably, John begins scrutining what covers his walls.

As a fanatic ritual, he revises his souvenirs, which are all to be found hanging on these walls. Pictures, more pictures and even more pictures. Within all of them, only three people can be seen; his wife Mary, deceased 11 years ago, Kevin, his son whom he has not seen since and who is now twenty-nine, and finally John…during much better days.

All the pictures are hanging in chronological order on the walls. If only one thing was to have some sort of order in this house, it is defi-nitely these pictures.

Let's begin with his wedding pictures. Mary was a very beautiful woman. She was petite but ravishing. Her five feet four inches was quite a contrast with John's six feet two. John was also very handsome at this period in life. He is also pictured with his family; his parents, his sister and two of his brothers. As usual, his eyes stop upon Simeon, his older brother with whom he had a close relationship. At this moment John becomes overwhelmed by solitude to the point of having difficulty withholding his emotions.

In addition to these pictures other ones can be seen which depict various trips taken with Mary and a few of their friends. He finds himself reliving these moments and can almost hear Mary's laughter. He surprisingly finds himself smiling and even occasionally laughing. Sometimes he talks out loud and answers to Mary's comments, which obviously come from his imagination.

In a fraction of a second he once again becomes melancholic, then takes more vodka and begins telling Pierre about another of his fishing trip or of some event in his past life. Pierre is the only friend who remains and which is not exhausted of hearing him recount the same stories over and again.

- *Look Pierre, there is the day where my buddies celebrated my promotion. Hey, it wasn't just anything you know! Special adviser to the International Affairs' Minister. I was only thirty-eight. My Mary was sure proud of her man. Kevin was only seventeen at the time but was already a man…Kevin…*

As time goes by, John says fewer comments. He shuts himself out more every time.

In 1984 Kevin left for college. Here, we can see Mary by his side, smiling and posing quite proudly in front of the new car they had just purchased for Kevin in recognition of his choice of career. Like his father, Kevin had decided on politics. This had not been imposed upon him; he had taken this decision on his own. The political arena had always fascinated Kevin since a very young age.

At this moment he is seated at the Chamber of Commons as regional candidate. Newspaper clippings show Kevin during his campaign and also with numerous crowds celebrating his victory.

This was the only way in which John could stay informed of his son's career due to the fact that since the terrible accident all contacts between the two of them have ceased.

The series of pictures give way to these numerous clippings and as though to force a miserable curse upon John, we can only see Kevin's name everywhere.

Kevin Chabot defends social assistants, Kevin Chabot fights against the governments anti-working politics, Kevin Chabot creates a funding program for the people illegally laid off by the wood transport company, etc etc. The name of John Chabot seems to have disappeared off the face of the earth. It is as though John's life ended where Kevin's began.

Finally, we come to understand. Away from all the other pictures and newspaper clippings which have become quite warn with the passing of time, other clippings can be found, dating back to the time of Kevin's ascension day in 1985, an event which John appears to indefinitely grasp hold of.

This other clipping read; "A government official kills his wife on his way home from a gala".

This is explained by the fact that John was known to have developed a dependence for alcohol. Mary had frequently suggested that John undergoes therapy but he always denied having a drinking problem.

To help Mary accept his denial John would frequently reply in a joking manner;

- *I will drink for as long as I will love you…. the day I stop drinking…then you'll have a problem my love.*

John could here himself stating this phrase that he had said repetitiously to Mary.

Then, his eyes stopped upon a copy of a famous newspaper showing a picture, which depicts his vehicle, crashed in a bridge support column and the emergency vehicles at the scene.

On that particular evening, John was returning home from a fund raiser organized for his political party when, due to having consumed too much alcohol, he lost control of his vehicle and crashed which resulted in the immediate death of the woman he had loved so deeply.

The other newspaper clippings, which follow, state all the details of this event and since John was a public figure, this story dragged on for several weeks afterwards in the news.

All the circumstances surrounding the accident up to the court procedures and including his sentencing could be read.

"John Chabot, Special advisor for the International Affairs' Minister found guilty of driving while under the influence having caused death…sentenced to five years without the possibility of parole"

It may seem as a severe sentence but this was not the first occasion that John found himself in court for driving while under the influence.

Once again John grabs hold of his bottle of vodka and talks to "Pierre".

- *She wasn't the one that was supposed to go Pierre. It's not her…I'm the asswhole…I'm the one who ruined her entire life…. I also ruined Kevin's life…*

Half asleep, John now has trouble talking…. even though he knows he's alone he attempts to keep conversing with his friend Pierre.

- *My son says I killed his mother…. it's not a lie you know. He says I'm only an irresponsible drunk and human trash. Kevin also says that if the people had really known me in those days, they would have never supported me. My son no longer wants to speak to me Pierre…. He says that I'm no longer his father…he says that I do not deserve to be his father. In fact, he simply says that I am…that I am…nothing!*

- *It's true...he does not drink at all and he is already a delegate at thirty-five whereas I was still only an advisor at thirty-nine.*

For a brief moment John falls asleep but in an abrupt gesture of the head he tries to remain awake and remember more memories with Pierre.

- *Hey Pierre.... start the movie...start the movie Pierre....*

John always concluded his ritual by viewing the recording of his wedding to Mary.

- *Never mind then.... I'll do it...worthless peace of crap.*

Then, John staggers towards the further end of the kitchen and starts the tape of his wedding day. Recorded on a 8mm tape without voices or music, the images begin rolling and John, still in Pierre's company, savors for the millionth time, the scenes of his union to Mary.

All of a sudden, John feels over-comed by an irrepressible sadness. The guilt causes a knot in his stomach. It eats him up as deep as his heart.... now exhausted and without being able to hold it in any longer, John bursts in tears and says out loud;

- *Forgive me Mary...forgive me...I miss you so much.... Please come and get me...come and get me.... I miss you so much...I want to be with you...please Mary....*

Unable to fight it any longer, John falls asleep on his couch still holding his bottle and while the film continues to play.

Second Chapter

With the monotonous sound of the camera's motor and accompanied by the tape spinning endlessly on itself, John falls in a deep sleep. The day slowly slips away to let the night come in and take over.

Outside, the impenetrable darkness of the countryside gently covers the wild scenery where John lives. No neighbors in sight, only trees and then more trees. Not even a stream or river could come break this stillness. John had built this home, which is only visited by the wind; with the few thousand dollars he had remaining upon his release from prison. Since then, he has not had the means to paint, decorate or finish the excavation of his property. At this time in life, John preferred to fall into a deep sleep rather than find himself isolated from the rest of the world, as was the case during the day.

When sleeping, John always kept a notepad at his side. He wrote his dreams on it and in moments where the alcohol had dissipated, he enjoyed reading them. Living with such an addiction, to the point of having difficulty remembering his own name, John felt more alive in his dreams. Also, he would frequently wake up, write his dream and then anxiously fall asleep again to live another one.

Such was John's life. Living in the past and feeding himself with the images of his dreams. This was much better than living the harsh reality that he would have to face otherwise.

Each and every night before falling asleep, John wished one thing, to dream of Mary. More often than not, she did come to him in them. John wrote about all of them, which in turn brought him the only warmth one would get from human contact.

That night, John heads in a dream as fantastic as the others he is accustom to having.

Mary is there. He is alone with her in a small village classroom. At the blackboard, a professor teaches them how to dress. This appears to be a very important lesson. John is seated next to Mary who is taking notes at an incredible speed. John barely has one phrase written whereas Mary has an entire book completed.

Also in this dream, John begs Mary to help him because he is afraid to fail the exam. Then, Mary looks at John and smiles softly. Knowing he is going to fail, John tries to grab Mary's notes and while doing so, she gets up and leaves the classroom. Mary leaves the room holding her diploma and he remains sitting there, holding onto her notes.

When opening the binder, in which Mary had taken so many notes, John only finds blank pages. Frustrated, he calls out for Mary to return but she does not.

Transported by the unreality of the dream, John instantly finds himself slaving away chopping wood and surrounded by the people of his village who are mocking him.

Immediately, John wakes up in a cold sweat and quickly begins writing all of these events and then mumbles to himself;

- *makes no sense…what could this mean…what's the connection. Stupid dream, there's no way of figuring it out after all…*

Then, as quickly as he awoke, John once again returns to a deep sleep and finds himself in another dream.

This time, an enormous beast confronts him. It is quite disgusting and has this yellowish liquid coming from its mouth. John feels threatened as the beast advances towards him. John believes his life is at risk but does not dare defend himself knowing this battle to be useless. The beast keeps advancing but John backs up, and then backs up some more and still some. The beast continues to advance towards John and is on the verge of reaching him when he notices a door behind him. Exhausted and without hope, John opens it but falls in space. In his fall he attempts to slow down but is unsuccessful. And, in an inexplicable moment, John says to himself;

- *Come on, it's only a dream…I don't have to worry. I'm dreaming…I know I'm dreaming…I cannot die…*

The dream abruptly stops there and John wakes up startled. His heart is beating extremely loud and rapidly. He has the impression it is coming out of his chest. John does not recall having ever felt so uneasy after a dream; he had never lived such an event. John feels oppressed. He becomes agitated and still under the effect of alcohol, he attempts to escape without knowing what he is escaping from. He trips on a chair and finds himself face first on the floor. Still in a state of shock, John grabs his pad and writes what he has just been through.

- *This is not normal…it has never happened to me before. Also, I was in my dream and I knew I was dreaming…it's really abnormal. I knew that I could escape from my dream…I…I would even say I could have changed the course of events had I thought of it.*

Having been quite traumatized by all of this, John stayed awake for the remainder of the night. He was haunted by the thought of falling asleep and reliving such events.

He kept watch of the time from three until sunrise. To fall asleep again is out of the question…at least for tonight. It was too risky.

John could feel the thirst coming over him. He turns towards the couch knowing that was where he last saw Pierre. He grabs hold of his bottle and as he comes to take a drink, fear overcomes him and he abruptly deposits it on his kitchen table.

• *No, not that, not that at all…I think I went too far this time.*

He then heads towards the kitchen sink, takes some water in an old pot and puts it to boil on his old wood stove. John treats himself to one of his rare coffees. He usually despises it! From three to eight o'clock, John must have gulped down at least ten coffees and smoked an entire pack of cigarettes.

At about eight, as usual, the "journalist" (this is what they called the person who delivers the newspaper in the countryside) honks in front of John's house to inform him that his paper has arrived.

John jumps up and rushes to get it while attempting to see the journalist's vehicle pull away.

He feels reintegrated within the real world and it reassures him to see life, as he knows it, still existing. The harsh emotions of the night have given him the desire to retake contact with reality; it's somewhat less shaky!

Before returning to the house John takes care of feeding his old mare and bringing her the daily care. He takes a little more time than usual to the point where even his tired mare wonders what has happened to her usually ungrateful owner.

Once returned to his house, John feels proud for having spent six hours without taking any alcohol. A sense of joy covers his face and he surprises himself by whistling an unfamiliar tune while brewing himself another coffee.

He looks at his friend Pierre and says;

- *My dear Pierre, you will spend the day alone. Today I'm going out with SANKA…and laughs vigorously.*

He then sits on a straight chair and begins flipping through the newspaper. He turns the pages while only reading the titles and adding his personal comments.

- *Here we've got a murder, a theft and a kidnapping…do you want more? Rising interest rates…but what the hell do I care about your stupid interest rates? Also, diminished consumption by the people…well there, I can say I do my part in that, and he begins laughing. Well well well, a rise in the price of vehicles…my Candy is gaining value.*

Feeling somewhat ironic and not concerned by the news, John continues his reading on the same tone…

- *The water reservoirs are at their lowest since the beginning of the season…it's like I always said…just drink alcohol…. it's good for the environment, ha ha ha! And now what else gentlemen reporter…nothing but garbage, only garbage, it doesn't really mean anything more than my worthless stupid dreams.*

Irritated by the social scramble, John flips the pages of the paper even quicker without reading any of it and then just grabs and thrusts it against the wall.

- *It's not even worth the paper it's written on!!*

As the paper falls to the floor, it opened to a certain page where a chronicle reads "What to do this weekend". This article grabs his attention, as he believes he now sees something that is not useless.

John once again feels taken by the adventure he lived the night prior.

- *This can't be for real, it's starting again except now, I'm not dreaming....*

John becomes agitated and looks everywhere. He grabs a fire log and begins swaying it through the air around him.

- *What is that...who's doing it! Who's there...huh, who's there!*

He then cautiously approaches the paper again and confirms what he had seen. It very well was written, black on white:

"Interpret your dreams yourself. Know how to retrieve their true meanings"

It was about a conferences being given by a dream specialist in a city found near St-Cecile.

John picks up the paper and reads attentively:

- *What is all this crap...let's see...*

Then John attentively reads the small publicity insert.

"You dream of people you have lost, you often have the same dreams. You have had the impression of being conscious during your dream, you believe your dreams can influence your decisions and help brighten your relationships…do not miss this conference…bla bla bla…"

- *Oh well, what the hell…I have to go.*

As John was making this discovery, a vehicle was approaching his home. Who could be coming to visit he thought. Nobody had dared set foot there for the past five years. John had become quite unpleasant, melancholic and grumpy, only succeeding in hurting those who dared approach him.

- *It's not possible, it just can't be. If this keeps up I'm going to start drinking again…for me it must be the opposite, I must be drunk when I'm not drinking!!! Oh no, not that worthless Simeon. What is he doing here after all these years? He's not going to get away with this. Look at him chew his dumb gum. To come and bother me…*

John takes place on his couch and prepares himself to go for some vodka should things get heavy between them

Simeon, his brother with whom he had such affinity ten years prior was coming to see him.

Simeon knocks, John does not answer. Simeon knocks again but there is still no answer.

- *John…. I know you're there, yells Simeon.*

Mumbling to himself, John answers:

- *If you know I'm there, then why aren't you coming in? We don't need an appointment here you poor idiot…*

Simeon pushes the door open and finds himself face to face with John.

They both remain silent. John doesn't even attempt to get up to greet him. Simeon takes a few steps and timidly takes a chance.

- *Hi there bro.*
- *Yeah....*
- *Listen...I'll come back...I only came...*
- *If you came to barrow money, you're out of luck but if you came to get drunk you didn't pick the right day for that either and finally if you came to get some news, well, they're the same as ten years ago, so...either you've lost your way and I show you it or you have bad news and trust me, I've had my share of that in this lifetime, so leave me alone and go bug someone else.*

Simeon feels like he has been caught off guard and somewhat angry faced with such meanness. He turns and prepares to leave. John scrupulously follows him with his eyes while wearing his cynical smile for his small victory.

Simeon is a shy person, He has become an agricultural producer quite envied in the region. He owns numerous properties and has the reputation of being somewhat prim and proper.

Once upon a time, John and Simeon stood as one. They did everything together. John had thrown him out after having left prison because Simeon had tried to bring John back on the right path of life. He tried every way possible to help John from feeling guilty of Mary's death and to fallow a disintoxication program.

Unfortunately, John had already sunken too deep and not even his closest brother's true love could have an effect whatsoever. He had pushed Simeon away with his mind set against being saved and therefore, out of shyness or uncertainty, Simeon did not dare to re-attempt this again.

- *If I heard correctly…you have stopped drinking, attempted Simeon still on his way out.*
- *Yeah…Yeah, I stopped drinking almost nine hours ago. So what do you think of that.*

Shyly, Simeon turns around and faces John.

- *Well at least…I'll be able to tell anyone I see that you did not take one drop the entire time I was here…with only that I'm sure nobody will believe me.*
- *That's it…you came to count the number of glasses I drink…well, go tell them that on certain days I even feel like eating my own shit and that sometimes I wake up hungry at night and eat rats for a snack…*
- *No John…I…in reality, I…*
- *You what…you wanted to know if the family's disgrace had not sunken even lower….*
- *That's not it John…you've always been my friend…you're not just a brother to me…you're my friend…and I find it sad that you have so much trouble.*
- *I want so much to help you but I can't. It's probably very selfish of me but I would be much happier if your life wasn't so difficult. I wouldn't want you to have spent twenty years slaving away and not get anything at the end.*
- *Don't worry about it. I quit a long time ago. Life is nothing but crap. It's a nice big pile of manure and the more time goes by, the bigger the pile gets.*

Simeon looks away realizing that it was hopeless.
John lets some of the tension between them settle down a bit and says:

- *Wait a minute, what did you say…*

- *Well, what I said…I was saying how I only wanted to help you John…*
- *No, no, not that…before, or after, I don't know…*
- *Well I said I would be happy if you didn't have it so hard…. and.*
- *No, immediately after that…*
- *I said…. that…you've been slaving away for so little…*

John interrupts him on these words and quite proud of his finding, continues…

- *That's it, I'm slaving away…*

John bounces off the couch to get his pad. Simeon looks at him quite worried and without understanding.

- *What is it John…*
- *That's it…slaving away…the village. the pad…Mary…the notes…the beast, the liquid…yes, it's becoming clear…*
- *John…are you okay John…*
- *Of course, I'm fine…I'm slaving too much for nothing…Hey, guess what…do you really want to do something for me, asks John quite excitedly.*
- *Well John, I'm afraid I don't understand…*
- *Don't try to understand, it makes ten years that I don't understand anything and I'm still breathing. You want to help me so we are going to do something you and I.*
- *Whatever it is John, just ask.*
- *Yes, that's it…tonight we are going out Simeon. You take me where I tell you.*
- *But John…your story frightens me a little…I think that you…*
- *No, you'll see. It's very simple. We're only going to a conference.*

- *Not one of those dumb liquor things where the guys are crying because nobody loves them and that life is nothing but garbage and not worth living…we've done them all John…it's useless*
- *No, no, it's something quite different. It's a surprise Simeon.*
- *We're not getting drunk either John. It's just that Rachel would be furious and she would blame it on you again…. you know.*
- *No, since we are also going to bring my Sanka along…*
- *Do I…know her?*
- *Of course, I would even say that you adore her.*

Third Chapter

On a hot and humid Saturday night in July, Simeon heads to pick up John, as promised. Behind the wheel of his Mercedes 560, Simeon fears arriving at John's house only to find him passed out on the couch.

Most certainly an alcoholic's recess, thought Simeon. He slows down and wonders if he should not just turn around. But, in the hopes that his brother, whom he has loved even during roughest of times, may have finally straightened himself out. Simeon arrives and proceeds down John's narrow entranceway.

A faint shadow can be seen from this gloomy home. The dense darkness that surrounds the house practically covers the headlights.

Simeon honks and within a few seconds John arrives quite assuredly holding his pad of notes from his dreams in one hand and a cigarette in the other. In a hurry John opens the passenger door to take his place.

- *Tonight…we're going to have a good laugh Simeon.*
- *At least tell me what it's all about.*
- *We are going to the school of life. We will finally know where to find the truth.*
- *…*

On the route to Trois-Rivieres, John and Simeon recall their best childhood memories. This gives Simeon the impression of finally finding his brother and John feels as though he has found life after having been dead for more than ten years.

- *John, do you remember the time we had to confront big Albert who had escaped in the cornfields?*
- *If I remember…do I ever! This big bull almost got me.*

John and Simeon burst out laughing while reliving this event.

- *We had rounded up all the cattle except this big Albert who refused to return to the stables and then you decide you're going to lure him by using the urine of a cow in heat!!!*
- *Yeah…so what, it worked, didn't it?*
- *Of course it worked. In the midst of autumn, Albert knew winter was approaching and that he would be put away until spring…not too stupid that Albert.*
- *Yeah…he never missed one.*
- *I never saw such a big bull…1200kg…*
- *You should have seen my face when I noticed him heading for me…*
- *Albert really had a bad attitude. You remember once when he had completely destroyed a hay wagon just to get some for himself…*
- *He sure destroyed allot of things this wild one…but deep inside I really liked this idiot. He protected his "mistresses"*
- *When I think about it…*

Simeon bursts out in laughter once again.

- *I sure would have liked to see you in my position. A bucket full of urine and big Albert who suddenly appears out of the corn, pissed, ready to mate with his new conquest! I had better move quickly…*

- *It was a good thing that you were near a fence...*
- *It's because this big jerk would have really gotten me...*

John and Simeon glance at each other and cannot contain their laughter.

- *I was so scared that I still kept a tight grip on the bucket of urine.*
- *Me, I was standing on the other side of the fence and I could hear you yelling "Albert, wo Albert,...Albert you big jerk"...It was dangerous but for some reason I couldn't keep from laughing, I lost control, just then I saw you suddenly appear in front of the fence holding onto your bucket of urine, I completely lost my breath.*
- *I had to jump at least four feet over that fence...*
- *With a bucket of urine too...*
- *Yeah well...let me tell you that I wasn't too careful with it...all week after that Albert kept sniffing me as though I was awaiting his favors...you know that you can wash yourself three times a day but during these periods, those animals can smell better than a bee.*
- *Oh, I'll always remember this.*

The forty-five minutes of traveling was much too short for the two brothers to exhaust all their memories.

- *Hey John, do you remember Nancy our cousin, on her wedding day, says Simeon recalling another anecdote.*
- *Do I ever...*

John suddenly becomes morose and sad.

- *Of course I remember...*

Simeon realizes he had committed an error and stops speaking. Harsh silence then invades them.

* *How could I forget? That's where I met…*

Simeon interrupts John before he has a chance to finish his sentence.

* *Forgive me John, I didn't mean to….*
* *Well it's okay, it's okay…just don't give me any of your lessons on morals.*

Once again, the two brothers feel a certain distance between them and both regret having mentioned this last souvenir which brought an end to their joyful but short-lived reunion.

* *Look, it must be there, says John, park here and we'll walk a little ways.*

They then headed towards this hotel, in downtown Trois-Rivieres, which is known for hosting various conferences.

In the entrance way we can observe several men and woman who are also there to attend the same conference. They are speaking in a low tome and appear to be middle-class. John feels as though he has unintentionally attracted some attention. He is quite in contrast with Simeon who is so neatly dressed. Simeon notices John's discomfort and attempts to reassure him.

* *Is this an evening for the stiffs anonymous or what!*

The both try to muffle their laughter and make their way to a certain table where inscriptions were being taken.

- *Are you here to attend the conference on dreams, questions a hostess?*
- *Unless you have something more pleasant to propose to me...*

Simeon gently elbows John and smiles at him to then continue the conversation himself.

- *Please excuse him miss. He is unable to resist the charm of such a pretty lady!*

Somewhat embarrassed, the young woman hands over a pair of tickets and requests the payment.

Once back to themselves, John and Simeon take place away from the group and whisper to each other in a petty tone.

- *You haven't really changed at all!*
- *Come on little brother, that's how we had fun in the old days.*
- *In the old days, as you put it, we were much younger.*
- *Yeah, that's it, we were young and had fun. We were young and lived. We didn't ruin our lives with allot of nonsense, rules and absurd ceremonies.*
- *I'm still living, John.*
- *False, you're not living any more than I. You're only surviving. You have a role and that's all. You don't really live. You don't know what it is to really live. To know the true meaning of life, one must die and I sure can tell you quite a bit about death. It's true that I don't really live life myself, in fact, I live it even less than you do because it is also true that I am dead but I feel the wind has changed and that now I'm being reborn into the real life.*

Simeon looks at him and appears to not have understood any of this gibberish.

- *Come, lets go, the conference will begin…maybe you will have a better understanding afterwards.*

The conference lasted for a little over three hours. John devoured every word the speaker said. During the entire evening, Simeon kept a smirk at the corner of his lips as to mock the speaker's findings. At times, he would take on a more serious appearance to not offend the others in the audience.

John got to a point where he no longer noticed his long lost brother's presence next to him. He was taking notes, writing as quickly as the host spoke and once in a while, he glanced at his pad where he had taken notes on his dreams.

Every so often, Simeon attempted to read John's notes but John had such a terrible writing!

Finally, the conference came to an end, it was late and Simeon had had his mind elsewhere for quite some time. Of course, he had been thinking of his wife and four children. Simeon did not make a habit of going out without them and by now Rachel is probably worried of John's influence on him.

- *So, what did you think of it little brother?*

John always amused himself by calling Simeon his little brother due to the fact that even though Simeon measured five inches less than him, he possessed a phenomenal built. Forty-inch shoulders, nineteen inches per arm width and iron hands.

- *Interesting. Not bad at all.*

Simeon gets into the car and takes advantage of this time to try and hide his deception while John waits for him to unlock the passenger door from inside.

- *What do you mean, NOT BAD AT ALL? Only not bad at all. But don't you realize.*
- *What is it that you want me to realize? Everybody dreams, it was entertaining, no more nor less.*

As Simeon starts the engine John grabs hold of his head with both hands and recaptures.

- *It's exactly as I said. You do not realize that you are living or maybe it's simply that you do not live at all.*

Silence....

- *Come on John, everyone dreams about different things but that does not mean each dream has a sense. According to this man we should pay more attention to our dreams than to events that take place during the day, when we're actually awake.*
- *But, that's exactly where the problem is. Our small brains, at least for the portion of it which we use, is insufficient to solve all our preoccupations and to find answers to all our questions. If we paid closer attention to our dreams, we would know what to say, what to do and what not to say and do. We would know our real goals in life, the reason why we are here, the reason why we meet such or such a person.*

The discussion was taking a very serious and philosophical tone but John's arguments did not appear to shatter Simeon's disbelief.

- *Well come on John. Listening to you, everything is explained in dreams, all the way to the most unimportant event.*
- *I could not have said it better myself...for example, this morning when you said "slaving away".*
- *So what, what's wrong with "slaving away", everybody says it.*

- *I agree, but I had seen this in my dream the night before. Here, look in my notes, it's written, look right here. You see.*

John shows him the pages where he describes having seen himself slaving away chopping wood while being laughed at by the locals.

- *And so then what. The fact that you see yourself "slaving away" in your dream and that I say it the following day is nothing to be afraid of.*
- *Even if I told you that I insisted, and prayed to all the Saints, that the meaning of it be given to me without delay.*
- *Simple coincidence.*
- *But Simeon. You are talking about great things as though they were chopped liver. Coincidences, as you put it, are part of the answers in relation to the dreams. Finally, it's not just unimportant coincidences but…of logical continuance, if I may say so.*
- *Okay, lets say that for this particular dream your theory holds up but you certainly cannot apply it to each and every dream.*
- *Of course not.*
- *Well, then, you see. A theory, my dear brother, to be scientific, you must be able to repeat it but it always has to give the same results. In the event of the contrary, it consists only of an observation without any scientific value. It then becomes a repertoire useful only for statistics.*
- *Simeon, I could not give the true meaning of each dream because, like you, I am too determined in only using the rational and analytical parts of my brain which blocks me from my true sense, being the irrational and intuition.*
- *If I tell you about a dream you will then be able to tell me its true meaning, even the craziest of them.*
- *No, unfortunately not. Remember when the speaker said that only the dreamer himself could give a dream its true meaning. Even the*

person closest to the dreamer couldn't achieve this without risking being wrong.

- *Yeah…I know, he did say that but….*
- *Yet, it's so simple. Even if you know the person and the language of dreams, you could never entirely know his/her spiritual state, his/her fantasies, ambitions or all the little well kept secrets…*
- *So this brings us back to what I have been saying all along. All of these people, just like the fortunetellers, abuse of people's naïveté.*
- *Unfortunately, there are so many. But, we are at a point in evolution where these fortunetellers are a necessity. Thanks to them, there are many people who try to strike it rich, but also thanks to them there are several people who try to solve this mystery of life but sooner or later they will realize that this can only be accomplished by themselves. But one thing is for certain, if these people are living a comfortable life style it's because the population, in general, admits that science, whether it be mathematical, political, social, etc, has not been able to answer their questions. Therefore, they are looking towards the "non science" but are on the wrong trail by trusting a third party. One day, and this day is near, you'll see my little brother, mankind will live by its own science. We will no longer have to depend on the different scientific facts. There will only be but one simple science; like a universal science, the evolutional science, the one that will permit us to know our true reason for being and all the rest will become secondary. Money, cars, furniture, jewlerery…all of that will no longer have any value. We will only have enough to live with, and no one will give you a single penny for all that's remaining.*

John appeared carried away, he simply would not give in and Simeon no longer dared argue with him about this. For John it was though he had just found what had been missing in his life. The missing piece to his puzzle had just manifested itself, as though he had just understood the reasoning to his disgust of the past ten years.

- *Hey, are you listening?*
- *Of course I am.*
- *You see Simeon, we are wrong to be working, to build a company, grow a family, to help people with this or that if in some way it has nothing to do with our path of life, with our evolutionary travel.*
- *And here I thought that all these past years all you did was sip some good wine.*
- *Alcohol was only my refuge Simeon. I had said no to this life which disgusted me but had not found a substitute. And slowly, all I had left to do was to think about life. I read, read some more and reread many books in regards to this. Each one of them had an element of truth and answer. Only printing the titles and authors of the books I read would in itself make a book of five hundred pages. But, at the end of all this there was still something missing for me and I was at the point where I believed that life would never reveal its mysteries to me and that from the beginning this had all been a huge joke by a crazy creator who has been mocking us for millions of years.*
- *Yesterday, when you came to see me, I had just lived the most horrifying night since Mary's death. But, since this morning everything has been happening so quickly that my brain is unable to assimilate it all. There's proof that once we leave the rational world our brain is unable to be up to the task.*
- *In any case John, I don't understand a tenth of what you are trying to tell me but what I do see is that since this morning, you have changed more than I ever imagined possible and in some way, that brings me joy.*

John and Simeon stop in front of John's home and bid goodnight. John appears gleaming of good humor where as Simeon is overtaken by these events. He can very well see that his brother has retaken hold of life in less than twelve hours but fears that it be brought on by an irratical thinking or a drunk's recess.

Simeon takes the road leading to his home while thinking about all the events that had just taken place. He's not quite certain what to make of all of it. Discussing dreams, coincidences and evolution was not quite his "thing", he who was so pragmatic and so close to the earth.

Fourth Chapter

That evening, John quickly fell asleep. He was exhausted by all these new emotions he had just lived.

As tired as he may have been, John was restless throughout that night, constantly moaning and occasionally letting out a few deep groans.

He frequently woke up to then fall asleep again and on several occasions he picked up his pad but his drowsiness kept bringing him back to a deep sleep, therefore was unable to write anything down.

In the midst of the night, at about two, John found himself in a very particular dream.

He could see himself sitting in a badly lit auditorium where a conference was being held. He appeared as though he was searching for someone. Unfortunately, it was so dark that he could not make out who was sitting there also. Suddenly, thanks to the host's projector gleaming, John finally recognized the person he appeared to have been searching for. It definitely was his son, Kevin.

Kevin was sitting in the front row whereas John found himself completely at the rear. He attempted to get Kevin's attention by whispering but failed.

As in a typically bizarre dream, John found himself holding his hand out and reaching Kevin's seat, regardless of the distance between the two. At this moment Kevin turned around and saw his father. In response to this John sinks himself deeply in his seat and smiles but Kevin rapidly becomes surrounded by a huge shell which prevents John from being able to reach him again.

Confronted by this awkward scenario, John leaves the auditorium by the back door. Then, by the magic of this dream, he finds himself play fighting with Kevin in a spacious pond where a nauseous odor was emerging.

Kevin quickly takes control of the struggled and projects John extremely high up in the air.

John feels himself being in free fall only to land in a lake where the water is extremely dirty and at which point the waves try to over-power him

He vigorously fights against these waves and succeeds in reaching the shore. In an instant, John feels very light and begins floating over the village.

He is abruptly brought back to reality by the noise of a window sway-ing in the wind.

He gets up to close this window and decides to turn on a lamp to make himself a coffee while attempting to remember this weird dream.

Coffee in one hand and pen in the other he writes down the slightest details of his dream while his cigarette burns itself out in front of him.

The following morning John gets up at the crack of dawn to dress himself in his best suit, actually, the one that is less worn out! He had not consumed a single drop of alcohol since that infamous night which had brought him into this fantastic world of the irrational. He was radi-ant and going about his home, alone, and singing like a child.

Reviewing the details of his last dream John found himself laughing.

He decided to clean up his home, beginning by washing the piles of dishes which had been accumulating for several weeks, swept the floors and opened a few windows to freshen the place and to let some daylight in.

The warm rays of the July sun quickly invaded the small room to actually give it some life.

John approaches his couch and leans over towards his old friend "Pierre".

• *My good old Pierre, still on vacation today. I've decided to take the big step. I must go see someone who undoubtedly awaits me.*

He stores the bottle of vodka in a cupboard and grabs his overcoat. He then makes a few steps but turns around and heads for the cupboards again. He grabs hold of his bottle of vodka and just holds it for a while without saying anything but eventually replies;

• *Wish me good luck, Pierre, I'm going to need it.*

John goes to the stables to prepare Candy and removes the tarp on his carriage. Usually he never removes this, even in summer because it keeps him more discrete towards the locals who never cease to watch his every move.

On the dirt road leading to the village, the fourth road that is, John proudly guides his horse and watches attentively for he locals' reactions towards him.

He did not have to wait very long to observe these first reactions.

Oliver, a breeder who lived in proximity from John, stops instantly in his tracks as he was preparing to cross the road, which separates his house from his stables.

John noticed him but continues on his route keeping his head high and proud. Passing by where Oliver was standing, John salutes him.

- *Hello there Mr. Baril, everything going okay?*

Oliver, taken by surprise, takes a few seconds to find his words. John had never addressed anyone before.

- *Yes,yeah, yeah, thank you…. Mr.…*
- *Chabot…Chabot,* says John amusingly.

John continues on his way with this great smile of victory on his face. Mr. Baril retuned to his home to tell his wife about this while only causing disbelief amongst his children.

- *There's something going on. He must have met a woman. Says Oliver.*
- *Drunks like that go from heaven to hell in no time. It won't last; replies Alice, his wife.*
- *No…. I've known him for ten years, ever since he's been living at the end of the road and…I've seen him take brief moments of dry spells but it has never been like this. Today, he actually saluted me, do you realize. He even spoke to me.*
- *Come on, you'll see, there's nothing to make a fuss over.*
- *No…there was something unusual…his eyes…he had some sort of twinkle in his eyes.*
- *Probably alcohol vapors shining in the sun.*

Oliver remained speechless standing at their kitchen window while observing John drive away and saluting everyone on his path.

John continued on his way and as though all was in his favor that day, he did not encounter any vehicles, which would have covered him in dust. Finally turning onto the asphalted road leading to the next village, John maintained his speed and appeared taking advantage of the beautiful sun to fill his lungs of fresh air.

He notices every bird, every small animal that crosses his path and even surprises himself at times by speaking to them. At certain moments, a bird will cease chirping and a dog from barking just to listen to him.

John is living an intense moment of closeness with nature and tells himself;

- *How could I have missed this for all these years? It was right here, all around me, and I didn't even notice it.*

In a moment of silence, John sheds a tear, overwhelmed by the joy he feels.

- *I was really dead. Forgive me God. Forgive me and...thank you for this beautiful scene.*

John was forced out of his daydreaming by the honking of a vehicle which appeared to approach him at a very high speed. He maneuvers Candy to free the roadway which, in some way, he had occupied in majority.

He replaced his headdress, which he had almost lost in this excitement and retakes control of his mounting.

The vehicle passes him only to immediately immobilize itself at approximately ten meters away.

It's Simeon. He exits his vehicle and bursts out laughing.

- *It's only that you are becoming a danger on our roads with that candy of yours, Johnny.*

In the old and better sdays Simeon called him Johnny as a friendly and familiar gesture.

- *Where were you, in one of your dreams again? Saying so to mock him.*

• *You really frightened me. No…well maybe yes, except that this time I believe I was dreaming while remaining awake. Simeon, can't you see all the beauty our planet has to offer? These birds so joyful, this grass so green, look at this stream which is so calming, and this maple tree over there, doesn't it appear to be spreading all of its energy towards the shrubs surrounding it. Also, this sun which is so pure and the sky so blue that it takes us beyond all our problems.*

Simeon glances at the surroundings and appears contemplating the decor but nevertheless, not at the same level of perception as John.

In fear of hurting his feelings again, Simeon remains in the same mind frame and adds;

• *You're so right Johnny, it's fantastic, almost divine. In any case, you seem in an even better mood than yesterday even though then you were overflowing with energy…I'm quite happy for you Johnny.*
• *I strongly believe that I am in the process of being reborn Simeon.*

Simeon cuts the conversation short and changes the subject.

• *Hey, tell me, are you on your way to repeat you gibberish to some poor innocent lady; states Simeon mockingly.*
• *Oh, I don't think about that anymore. No, this morning I woke up with this feeling that it was time I take a big step.*
• *Oh yeah, now you've peaked my curiosity John. May I know what it's all about?*

John becomes quite nervous and rolls his hat a thousand times in his hands.

- *Well, I don't know if it's a good idea but it won't stop haunting me since this morning, it's actually like a very strong intuition that I'm unable to get rid of.*
- Laughing, Simeon adds; *be honest, it's much more an impulse than an intuition. And what is the name of your "little impulse".*
- *It's not funny at all Simeon. I'm just as nervous as when I asked Mary to be my wife but now it does not involve a woman.*
- *Then, it involves…a man…*
- *Yep, quite a man too…a real one…I'm going to see Kevin…*

Dead silence places itself between the two men. Simeon is quite aware of the image that Kevin has of his father, and of the grudge he holds against him.

As for John, he is not unaware of this but believes in his magnificent star, which has been guiding him for the past forty-eight hours.

- *Well…I believe he's at his office, in St-Pierre. Actually I will be seeing him this afternoon regarding business on agricultural zones, says Simeon.*
- *Yeah…I didn't call before hand but I knew he'd be there. Probably an intuition. I would like him to at least say hello, that's all. After all this time…*

John's lips begin trembling and he desperately attempts to retain his tears. Simeon becomes uncomfortable and attempts to reassure him.

- *You know, Kevin has matured quite a bit in the past ten years…He also lived some difficult moments so I'm certain that he doesn't see things as he used to.*
- *Of course, continues John while attempting to hide his pain.*

- *Come on, everything will be fine. Go see your son the Deputy, hold him tight in your arms but don't forget to tell him how much you love him.*
- *Thanks Simeon, we'll talk later.*

Simeon slowly returns to his vehicle, worried that this event may only push John back to his drinking habits.

- *Heh, you know you can count on me at all times, day or night…*
- *Yes…says John in a week tone.*
- *Call me…. big brother.*

These two last words brought a smile to John's face. Simeon had never used these words simply because he did not want to give in to John when he mocked him by saying Simeon was his little brother.

At about nine o'clock, John arrived in St-Pierre in front of a very modern building. This building held a few offices on the top floor and some boutiques on the main floor.

He first goes into a general store to purchase an item he absolutely wanted to bring with him.

With great difficulty and nervousness, John makes his way up the staircase leading to Kevin's office. At that same moment two strangers are descending this same staircase. Caught off guard by John's presence, they awkwardly salute him.

John finally arrives on the top floor, checks out the listing board and locates Kevin's office number. He feels pride when reading the name of his son

"Office of Deputy Kevin Chabot; No. 2"

John makes his way down a short hallway and hesitates once he finds himself in front of Kevin's office.

He eventually decides to enter and timidly addresses the receptionist.

- *Pardon me miss…*

The receptionist looks up at him and suddenly appears uneasy. Everyone is known in this area and therefore who would not know John Chabot.

- *What…. what can I do for you…Mr.…sir?*

Even uneasier than her, John continues.

- *I would like to…may I speak with…is my…is the…deputy present.*
- *Of course, please have a seat, I'll advise him of our presence.*

Before leaving her desk the young woman attempts to retake control of the situation by offering John a coffee.

A padded door separates Kevin's office from the reception area. In this environment it is of great importance that the subject of conversations remain in the office.

In his office Kevin has difficulty believing the news his secretary just brought him?

- *You must certainly be mistaken miss.*
- *No, it really is your father. Out of tactfulness I did not request his name but I would recognize him amongst millions of people.*
- *But what could he be doing here. Tell him…tell him that I'm busy and that…that I'll call him.*
- *But Sir…*
- *But what…this is not a family reunion office, I must see to my professional occupations.*
- *Certainly, but he appears quite sad…and so lost.*

- *My father has always been lost, he knows nothing but that, being lost. Go on, I don't have a second to lose listening to his old complaints. If I let him do it once he'll always come back for more.*
- *So…I get rid of him?*
- *That's it…get rid of him, throw him out, do what you want but just get him out before anyone recognizes him.*

Uncomfortable, the receptionist returns to the waiting area to execute her orders but John is no longer there. She notices a brown paper bag on her desk containing a card, which was not signed.

Having noticed the length of time it was taking for Kevin's response, John knew it would not be in his favor.

After having searched for John the receptionist returns into Kevin's office to inform him of her findings.

- *Sir, he has already left. I'm positive I asked him to take a seat…he left a…*

Kevin glances out his office window and observes his father leaving the building carrying a heavy weight upon his shoulders. He grumbles and advises his secretary that he is leaving the office.

- *I will be absent for a few minutes, take all my messages and do not cancel any appointments.*

Emotionally and hopeful, she acknowledges by a head tilt and wipes a tear which shows exactly how she feels in regards to this situation.

Kevin rushes down the staircase and manages to catch up to John.

- *What did you want, says Kevin in a very distant and informal manner?*
- *Oh…Kevin…no…never mined. It's not worth it. I must have lost my mind for a moment actually believing you may have forgiven me.*

- *Oh father, we're not going to start that again.*
- *It does not consist of starting anything as you say, but to put an end to it.*
- *We're not alike you and I...we don't think alike, we don't act alike, we don't sleep alike, we don't eat alike, we certainly don't talk alike...*
- *But Kevin, nevertheless, the blood running through our veins is alike.*

Kevin senses that this is quickly becoming an argument and absolutely refuses this to be a subject of gossip in the town.

- *Ok,...wait, I have about thirty minutes. If you are still capable of drinking anything other than alcohol, there is a small quiet cafe two streets away; I'll meet you there in two minutes.*
- *I'll request a secluded table no doubt; states John guessing Kevin's uneasiness.*

This get together only lasted fifteen minutes. John informed Kevin of his deep regrets regarding Mary and admits that all his life he never really knew how to truly be himself. For John this was a sincere confession he was making to his son. He informed him how he had been living in hell for the past ten years. At certain moments Kevin retained his emotions refusing to let any sign of sympathy show.

John monopolized the conversation. Also, he recognized the pride he felt for his only son. Despite Kevin's feelings, John informed him that he will always love him and he understood his reaction. Finally, he quickly explains to Kevin what he has been living lately and admits that he would want this to last for the remainder of his life. He also confides the fact he had not consumed any alcohol for the past two days and that this had been his record for the past ten years. He states he is taking it one day at a time and for the moment he did not feel any urge for some. He continued by stating what he was presently consuming was the nature surrounding him and of life itself.

Kevin listened without interrupting and concluded by stating:

- *Listen father, there is a world which separates us. If things are look-ing up for you, then so be it but don't count on my visiting and it would also be preferable that the people don't see you hanging around here…you understand…politics…*
- *Of course…politics…the image.*

Kevin turns his head and glances outside, his look empty and some-what bothered.

- *It is not I who created this situation dad. You had your chance so don't come and compromise mine.*
- *I know, I know. Go, you must be in a hurry.*
- *Listen well, you wanted to talk to me, it's done, I listened. I'm happy for you and I hope it brings you comfort. Now, do as you please but let me live my life in my own way. Regarding us, it's over, there's nothing left to gain of it. Anyways, I must go. Please excuse me. Good luck father but don't have any dreams regarding me, you will only be disappointed.*

Nonetheless, Kevin bids goodbye to his father with a handshake, but it was without any sentiments.

John smiles at him but does not add anything further. He remains seated there and reviews their conversation. He would have liked this to be warmer, closer but on the other hand he felt some form of relief, almost a liberation. In spite of the humiliation this caused him, he suc-ceeded in meeting with his son and above all…he was sober doing so! Then, Kevin's last phrase came back:

- *"…Don't have any dreams regarding me, you will only be disappointed"*

- *If only he knew everything.* Says John to himself smiling.

Fifth Chapter

Five months had gone by since this reunion between John and Simeon. Since then John remained alcohol free and decided to fix up his home.

The exterior has been recovered in aluminum siding, the barn freshly painted and the interior of the house repainted in much softer colors.

More furniture was also added, it was used but in good shape. This brought some new life and filled certain empty spaces. Of course John did not have the means to afford all of this since he is living from social assistance.

His reputation had proceeded him, which destroyed any chance of him ever finding employment again in the area.

Therefore, all his new repairs had been offered to him by Simeon.

As the holiday season was quickly approaching, John felt it be the right thing to invite Simeon for dinner. Out of politeness, he had also invited Rachel and the children even though he already knew that only Simeon was going to show.

It was Saturday, December 14th and John had prepared the dinner. He also set the table but only for two.

At twenty hundred hours, as planned, Simeon arrives at John's home, alone.

John had been burning some incents to perfume the place and had set some soft music to create a relaxed atmosphere.

The lights were dimmed and John rushed to meet Simeon upon his arrival.

- *Well…hello there Simeon, you appear to be alone…*

Noticing the two place settings, Simeon added.

- *As you probably expected…Listen you can't blame Rachel…*
- *I know, she is more of the prudent type.* States John smiling.

John invites Simeon to remove his coat and to join him in the living room.

- *Simeon, I don't know how I'll ever thank you, I could never repay you for everything you have done for me. The paint, the furniture, the barn…I could never repay you…*
- *Come on, you know that you and I have stopped counting these things a long time ago.*
- *Yeah, in the old days it was each our turn to pay but now it will more than often be your turn.*

Simeon becomes melancholic and pensive.

- *Your memory must be some short John. Without you…we would no longer have our little Amelie.*
- *Oh,…there he is bringing that up again.*
- *No, it's true John, she could have died then.*
- *I was only there by coincidence, that's all. I did what anyone would have done. You don't owe me anything for that.*
- *In any case, you had courage.*

- *It was more like unawareness; we could have both remained there. More or less the instinct of wanting to save a fellow human being.*

John and Simeon cease to talk, reliving this horrifying scene where John saved Amelie from a burning barn.

Amelie was trapped under a pile of wood and the flames would have reached her in less than a minute. John had freed her just in time for her to run out of the burning barn. Just as she was running out an explosion occurred and nobody ever believed they would see John Chabot again.

A few seconds later, John crawled out of the burning remains and was saved by others present. He had received a large piece of metal which remained implanted in his side. This required two surgeries and three weeks hospitalization.

- *Be reassured of one thing John, Rachel remembers this…if she's not here this evening it's only because she's worried the children…*
- *I know…I know…that one day they'll come…*
- *She doesn't admire you any less.*
- *Come on, all that is in the past. Let's take a seat at the table and have you taste the best pancakes ever.*

During the supper, John and Simeon discussed John's new life. There were very few comments about anything else. On a few occasions, out of politeness, John appeared interested in Simeon's business and family matters. Just as quickly the discussion would again revolve around John's findings.

- *Do you still write your dreams?*
- *Of course. You see, all I do is that. I don't play golf, I don't do sports, I don't drink anymore, I don't smoke anymore, I don't even have sex anymore…therefore it kind of keeps my mind busy.*

Simeon looks around and notices an impressionable library. Books on psychology, some discussing different religions, a few on spirituality, a few novels and a series of volumes written by the same author. By looking at this name Simeon believes he may be Russian or something of the sort.

- *Tell me, have you read all those books?*
- *Most of them, there are some that I still have not completed. When it doesn't "click", as we say, I don't waste time on it. It's either too out there for me or of no value what so ever.*
- *What are they about, in general…?*
- *Oh, this and that. Story tales about drunks unable to change.* Says John with a smile.
- *You know what, since you brought me to that conference on dreams, last summer, it got me thinking and I believe that there is actually some truth in what you were saying.*
- *Oh…you've got to take some and leave some. We must not direct our lives solely on our dreams. But, it's a good source of information and frequently useful advice.*
- *I had also begun writing down my dreams and became vigilant in regards to coincidences which followed these dreams but Rachel quickly noticed this and did not approve. She says that it is foolish nonsense and actually thought I could be a member of a cult.*
- *Well you know these are very unusual things, which usually put people on their guard. They are things that must be kept to oneself. Others will believe you are crazy if you tell them your secrets. It's almost like talking about reincarnation, life after death, extra-terrestrials, etc…What people cannot see, nor touch, nor hear, nor taste, it's all placed in the same basket and become taboo subjects which cannot be discussed, at least not seriously.*
- *And yourself, what do you think about it?*

- *Hum…you mean what I know. I know many things Simeon. I know many things repeats John in a withdrawn and pensive manner.*
- *Like what, for example?*
- *Oh, you'd be surprise and besides, it would be much to long to explain. Furthermore, one has to discover this by himself.*
- *You mean that all we have to do is read these books, that's it?!*
- *Absolutely not. There's nothing in these books. The books are sufficient enough to have you understand that you'll never know anything unless you work on yourself. You read, read some more…and read even more, one day you realize you have nothing in front of you…you believe it to be completely worthless, gibberish from old wise men gone mad, and you can read all you want…you're not touching anything tangible.. then, all of a sudden your soul overturns, you sort of become mad yourself. You tell yourself you have just opened an invisible door on something just as invisible but which appears to be existing. A short while later you realize that you have begun without really wanting it, by accident.*
- *Begun what?*
- *Working on yourself.*
- *Working on myself?*
- *Of course, that's it. We forget to work on ourselves. We want to help others, we build ourselves a house, a family and bla bla bla and bla bla bla…and what does it bring us exactly!*
- *But it's useful anyways.*
- *That's it, it's only useful, not necessary! One is not born basically to one day build a house. We don't put up with all this crap to arrive at sixty-five with a house, a car, a cottage and a small pension plan. It would be too ridiculous…*
- *I don't quite understand John. What are we doing here then if not to…to do our time?*
- *Poor old Simeon, I'll tell you what you're here for…*

John gets up, takes a few steps and slowly turns towards Simeon, staring at him and without moving;

- *My dear Simeon…you're here to get yourself out of the crap you've gotten yourself into millions of years ago.*

Simeon bursts out laughing, incapable of reacting any other way.

- *Poor John, I was expecting anything else but that. You're not serious, millions of years? I probably won't have enough of this lifetime just to repair the mischief of my childhood.*

John and Simeon burst out laughing and cannot control themselves to the point
of being short of breath.

- *But what are you trying to say. You're telling me that I'm carrying out a sentence of an entire lifetime, a lifetime that lasts…several life times…I don't understand.*
- *A bit of that. You know, the real life is not the one which we are presently living. We are only at one stage. Each person is a part of a whole and all of it must reach a certain level before being able to go further. Like a chain, which is as strong as its weakest link, society cannot move ahead until everyone has worked on his own evolution.*
- *It's as though you are telling me that even if I double all the links in a chain but forget one, the chain still won't be stronger than before?*
- *Exactly, we must all participate in our common evolution.*
- *By each his own evolution?*
- *That's it. Take this for example. We go to school, we do our first grade, then we attain our objective, we pass to the second grade and then the third, and so on until university. Also, there are superior levels beyond university such as research and development.*

- *As a society, if everyone was content with achieving only the first few grades of schooling, we would not be very advanced.*
- *Evidently!*
- *A majority of people must then give the best, the push required and if you notice, the societies which are the most advanced in technology are the ones who permitted the majority of their citizens to have access to the most schooling possible. But, if only a small percentage of their population had attained this level, they could not fully exploit their intelligence because they have to act in accordance with what is accepted at the level that the rest of the population is arrived. Otherwise, they would have to leave to join societies that are at the same level as them.*
- *I don't quite follow you on that one.*
- *In two words…can you imagine what good a lawyer, an architect and an engineer would be if we sent them to the African jungle where the tribes are still hunting with spears?*
- *Yeah…I understand but can't we help them…civilize them?*
- *That's it…now we're back to our main subject.*
- *I think we're way off by now.*
- *Not at all. At an evolutionary and spiritual level, it's identical as on this physical plan, the intellectual. Each has to do his levels of learning and the more that will be advanced, the more we will be able to exercise our new powers, our new faculties. We must, each and everyone, see to our own evolution and when an occasion presents itself, help a few others. At least, that is what the general idea of these books is.*
- *New powers, new faculties?*
- *It appears to be properties that mankind possesses but which has not been exploited yet.*
- *Simply, we are there to evolve!? But you told me it was because I got myself in some crap millions of years ago. I don't understand exactly.*

- *Mankind, according to what I have read, is a part of what we call God. In its path, this divine part which inhibits all of us, came on earth millions of years ago, to live this bodily experience. Through this experience which restrained him, mankind had to by the forces of efforts and achievements, live several experiences and acquire multiple knowledge to perfect its evolution. This done, he had to also love this planet, give it life, create structure to embellish life here and participate in the development of the other species also found here.*
- *It didn't turn out very well, did it?* Says Simeon jokingly.
- *Yep, mankind became to materialistic, concentrating only on the physical level becoming to attached to matter. Mankind made it poisonous and got further away from his divine part, he has continued his flight at too low an altitude, as a matter of fact. Mankind instead, attempted to dominate the other species and use them for their own purposes and therefore built himself a world quite imperfect and too "human" which is a menace to him more every day. He has poisoned the air which he breathes, has changed the configuration of the forces of nature that are on the verge of replying, and be careful when this does happen, it will hurt tremendously. All the forces of nature deployed to manifest its disgust towards mankind who has mistreated it for millions of years; I prefer not to be here at that moment…He has disobeyed the universal laws by believing he is the owner of this planet when in fact it is only on loan to him. Mankind has done this by forgetting his divine portion. That is where we all got ourselves in big trouble. Therefore, throughout the millenniums, mankind has detached himself from the divine level and began regressing, "dis-evolving".*
- *And now…*
- *Now…we are there. We must put it in reverse, and quickly, very quickly. We must bring back the pendulum, retake our spiritual evolution. We must return to our real sources, get in contact with it and right our wrongs towards humanity and life in general. They are*

considerable Simeon, it's a disgrace for the entire human race. We have ruined everything, destroyed, massacred, wiped out, raped and mocked. The animals have nothing to reproach themselves and truly only have as "animal", their name. We must confess, judgment day has arrived, and the party is over.

- *So that is why we have to work on ourselves?*
- *Yes…everyone for himself, as soon as possible and with the greater number of people possible, and one day we will have reversed the forces…if it's not already too late. We must bring back the pendulum.*
- *So basically, we are here for two reasons, find our divine evolution and repair our errors.*
- *You have said it all in one simple phrase.*
- *Therefore, according to you, all the diseases, aids, hurricanes, earthquakes, the flooding, the dry spells…all that is a response from nature itself.*
- *Divine…the divine nature Simeon.*
- *What about the cell phones, the planes, the asphalted roads, cars…we should do what, get rid of them. Come on, we're not to start back with climbing up trees to get some coconuts, are we?*
- *Of course not but we must continue the technical evolution while, simultaneously respecting the laws of nature. There exists several non-polluting resources, non destructive which have yet to be discovered yet alone used. We will discover them only when we let this high spiritual dimension intervene. We are only searching in the matters that presently surround us. There is a treasure to discover on a higher level. We must stop destroying everything. There are presently several movements that watch this and acts accordingly and which also keeps a watchful eye on the destructors but their forces are still too wide spread. We must help them.*
- *Your story sounds a little contradictory. You want man to continue to advance in technology but at the same time he must cease improperly*

using the earth's resources and only use..."green" *resources. How would you build cars...recycled or non-polluting, for example!?*

- *Of course man has reached a maximum and the advancement of science has become arduous, difficult, and expensive. There is a certain slowdown of the so-called technological and scientific evolutions, as we know it to be, contrary to what they want us to believe. To simply find a vaccination for a certain illness we must spend millions and millions of dollars and wait over 10 years. You find that quick you? Can you then say that science is advancing quickly, that it has no more secrets? Bull, the science is stuck, constipated; it is on the verge of yelling forfeit. Not sooner have we found a solution does another problem surface, and so we search for another solution. We only react. Nowhere do we really act. We read on the physical level because we do not see where the problem really originates. They come from a superior level and the most ironic of it all, is that we are the ones who create and call upon them. We cross our fingers and hope that it will be the last one and that has been going on for two thousand years. My definition of man has become as follows: "an intelligent animal who acts like a beast!" Whether it be on a political level, scientific or even social, it's always the same thing, we only react. Mankind is going to have to find new ways to advance. The metal era has just ended. The industrial revolution has reached its maximum. This route has proven its incapacity to take us further. It is running out. We are facing failure. Dead end, bus station...everyone gets off!!*
- *But mankind has never ceased advancing. He has even survived over millions of other animal species, vegetable and mineral that have not been able to adapt.*
- *Do you know that every year, hundreds of species disappear? Man, him, is still there.*
- *What you are saying is true but the mistake that man is presently committing is that he believes he has reached his peak as a specie. If*

it's true that man has come from an unknown amphibian to become homo sapiens, then homo erectus to finally become the human, as we know it to be today, why have the arrogance that in five thousand years our descendants will not have the privilege of having more evolved than what we are today. It would be slanderous, unforgiving and of total disrespect for all those preceding us and those succeeding us. This insinuates that we are the unchanging perfect result of several millions of years of evolution.

• *Yeah…seeing it this way…*
• *Even more than that, how could we affirm being the only beings of this galaxy having reached the highest level of evolution that can exist in this era?*
• *You're talking about…*
• *Extra-terrestrial life of course.*
• *Yeah…a proof by deducting facts.*
• *Exactly. Lets only go about four hundred years. We claimed, and I emphasize on "claimed", as we claim many other things, that there were other continents besides the one our ancestors lived on. But from there to bringing sufficient proof we had to dare believe and discover it. Once there, they did not only discover this new land, baptized it America, but we have also found other human beings, less evolved of course. We did not wait for any proof that this land did exist before going to find it and besides, what did we base this on; on the "impression" of a man who was viewed as mad becoming a historical hero. In reverse, why, today or in a couple of years, should foreign explorers not also discover us? A Christopher Columbus of modern times, making us inter-galaxy tribes considered not too evolved! An inter-galaxy Viking! Believing that only our planet, only our galaxy can be inhabited has become an euphemism. Maybe we'll be the ones to discover other extra-terrestrial beings less evolved or more evolved than us but at the end, to deny this possibility becomes as narcissist as believing we are the perfection of a specie which cannot be improved upon.*

I'm talking about other planets but I could just as well be referring to these beings existing on another dimensional level such as space-time and on this planet of ours too. A parallel world, I guess.

- *But tell me, where do you get all that…*
- *Listen, I've read, I've assisted to a thousand and one conferences, I've watched and attempted to understand the non-visual of several movies, and finally, in front of nothing, I ended by finding the true source of information.*
- *Your dreams…*
- *Yes…my dreams. It's a means like many others but it is one too.*
- *If what you say is so true, why haven't we heard about it yet.*
- *Because…because it's a fearsome and powerful weapon. More powerful than the atomic bomb, more powerful than anything you can imagine.*
- *And…the international powers don't use it because…*
- *Because it has not yet been revealed to them, that's all.*
- *I see, only you have the guard of it. It'll be quite nice on the evening news.*
- *No. It's not that one has the guard of it or not, it's simply that not just anyone can have access to it.*
- *Just a minute there…everyone dreams, correct?*
- *Yes, everyone dreams but here again, one must know how the world of dreams is governed.*
- *Ah…besides all this there are laws to be able to dream.*
- *Exactly. During the day when you're awake, laws and rules of all sorts surround you…no?*
- *Well…. yes.*
- *For example, we would not authorize you to attend to sick people if you did not have the necessary studies. On the other hand, if you are a doctor, and you heal the sick and that you abuse of your powers, you will end up by losing this privilege, no?!*
- *Evidently!*

- *Well, in this parallel world of dreams, it works in the same way except...*
- *Except what...*
- *Except that the only ones who can access it are those who, at no moment, can utilize the ultra powerful powers of this world for wrongful use on this world of ours, the awakened world if you prefer.*
- *And what if a wise guy succeeds to slip into the system...and grab's some information to bring back to "our" world?*
- *Impossible. It is as easy for a camel to fit in a needle's hole as it is for an impure soul to enter this kingdom...or something of the sort.*
- *Hey wait.... you're reciting the bible now.*
- *And why not. Where do you think these things come from, the bible, the coran, and all the others like that?*
- *Well, if we rely on what we say...*
- *That's it;...we must certainly rely on it. But, were Mohamed, Jesus, and Buddha so different from us?*
- *Well...*
- *Of course the answer is "no". Absolutely not except...except that they already had access to the universal information, to the so-called "divine" laws.*
- *Therefore I am a...Jesus;* interrupts Simeon jokingly.
- *You are...you are a Jesus in power. We are all a Jesus, a Buddha...Gods but we excel in proving the contrary by being cruel to our neighbors, by cheating our spouses, by killing our enemies, by envying the wealthy, by repulsing the poor etc etc.*
- *In a very complicated way you just simply want to tell me that I should attend Sunday mass and I will became a Jesus of Nazareth.*
- *You know Simeon, and you are well in position of knowing that one doesn't simply have to take dance lessons to become a dancer or to learn the law to become a judge. You have to practice, put in action, feel and live what you have learned. The mistake we do is that we remain content in reading the bible to believe it. You have to live the*

bible, you have to become a living bible and then, only then you will be able to cross over to the other world and participate in the advancement of the one whom you really are.
- *Boy…you impress me with what you are saying now. It could simply be entertaining but I have the impression that there is actually something there.*
- *Well, look at that.*

John hands Simeon a dozen forty-five-page manuscripts.

- *What is that?* Says Simeon quite intrigued.
- *That is the pure truth. In these registers you will find all the mysteries of life. The origin of man, his reason for being, his condition, his role in regards to the other animal species, vegetable and mineral species, his connection with the "divinities" as we put it.*
- *In these manuscripts, the paralytic as the autistic, the poor, the schizophrenic, the depressive, the politician, etc etc; they will all find the explanation to their human condition. The secrets about the sicknesses such as cancer, the plague or aids are all revealed. These suffering all have a reason for existing and we should not be looking for a cure but for their reason of being and destroying that. You see, we must act instead of reacting. All the answers to any questions you may have are found in them.*

Completely lost, Simeon attempts to twist the conversation into a joke.

- *Are you thinking of publishing…?* Asks Simeon to tease him.
- *Not for the moment.*
- *And why is that?*
- *For various reasons but especially because…I don't understand a word of what's written in them…states John ironically.*
- *But…*

- *I know that everything is there but I have to decipher it. I transcribed the answers brought to me by my dreams but the language of dreams is so different from ours, one day I'll find the connection…I don't know how…but it must happen.*
- *Okay…I see…*
- *No kidding…you can laugh but one day, I'll probably be dead and so will you, they will read these phrases like we learn mathematics today or philosophy.*

On a sarcastic note Simeon continues.

- *I would sure be nervous in keeping such a treasure in my home…wouldn't a bank security box be better…. don't you think?*
- *Tell yourself one thing; absolutely nobody would manage to grab these manuscripts without putting himself in danger.*
- *After the "adventure of the lost arc…the night of the rubberish manuscript"…*

John stops and looks at Simeon as though he regretted having confided such deep feelings with him.

Simeon becomes uneasy and attempts to reroute the subject to a serious note, believing he may have pushed it a little overboard.

- *Listen John, I may appear to be taking this as a joke but it's only that I don't believe I'm ready to accept everything you have been telling me. What you have been saying makes sense but it's too much, and out of the ordinary…I believe that I may just simply be overwhelmed.*
- *Don't worry about it. I'm used to it. It makes ten years that I have been living alone with this secret. I always hope to convince someone and enlarge my circle. At the very bottom of things Simeon, you are not just overwhelmed, you are afraid.*
- *Not at all.* States Simeon somewhat insulted.

- *Yes Simeon, we are all frightened of losing our little humanoid status by accepting that finally we have just become mollusk supplied with an intellect so great that it has wiped out all other sensory possibilities, lets just call them "extra-sensorial".*

Simeon, feeling vanquished and unable to respond, prepares his exit.

- *Listen John, I feel quite interested in listening to what you have to say but...*
- *You're afraid...*
- *Yes...I fear that you may have joined some kind of religion or even a cult...*
- *A cult with only one member Simeon...*
- *But what if you were able to...*
- *To recruit members....*
- *Yeah,...as a matter of fact...*
- *Absolutely not...I'm only doing this for myself. You see this house, it is my temple. You see these manuscripts, they are only my bible. You see anything else....?*
- *No, not really.*
- *I told you earlier, you cannot learn this from books, you cannot learn this from others, and it absolutely cannot be taught. Therefore, it's impossible to form a group what so ever. I would be offered a thousand dollars a second to teach this and I would refuse.*
- *First of all, because money, I have some when I need some. Secondly, because I would accomplish nothing...and especially because it is quite incomplete at the moment.*
- *Each and everyone must accomplish this on his own. But, all this said, it makes me feel good to basically talk about it, at risk that it wakes up your own questions within yourself. But then, we would be two except that neither one of us can help the other; we could only*

understand the other. Yeah…but I'm starting to have a headache and Rachel is going to be worried.

- *Go, I've already said too much.*

After a few salutations and unimportant remarks on the winter weather, Simeon hands out a handshake to his brother, which he knows he has finally found even with the great difference in their beliefs.

John feels the same joy as his brother and after having pretended he wanted to play fight, holds him tight in his arms and bids good-bye on these last words:

- *No matter what you are, who you are, where you come from, where you are going…you will always be my little brother…*

Simeon leaves John by gently giving him three brotherly slaps on his shoulder as to demonstrate his encouragement.

Sixth Chapter

Once Simeon departed, John returns to his manuscripts and overlooks them with satisfaction.

On some occasion, he shows a faint smile at the corner of his mouth and at other moments becomes serious.

He reviews his unfinished work while nodding his head as one does when reviewing school notes.

Exhausted by this evening rich in emotions and by the late hour, John falls asleep on his couch.

That night, John experienced two dreams that were worthy of being noted. In his first one, John finds himself in the company of Mary.

They are sitting at a large table surrounded by an immense garden where the flowers and trees appear to have come from a fairy tale. He is sitting at one extremity and Mary at the other.

There is nothing set on the table but it is covered by a white cloth. In the center of it shines a beautiful bright white light that glimmered tremendously but still, was not blinding.

They are discussing without even opening their mouths. They each comprehend the other's thoughts immediately and return their answers in the same manner.

- *Thank you Mary for everything you have done for me.*
- *I have done nothing John, you must be proud of yourself.*
- *But without you, I would not understand everything I now know.*
- *Don't be foolish, I contented myself of simply being present as to make certain you did not lose your way.*
- *Even that.*

They communicated with harmony, relaxed and with a soft slow tone.

- *I've used you just as much as you may have taken advantage of my presence John. We have to help each other mutually, do you remember?*
- *I don't quite follow you…*
- *But yes, don't you remember. Once we returned to this world you invited me to share a part of your path, otherwise you would have had trouble making it.*
- *Oh Mary, you are taking me so far back.*
- *It was hundreds of earthly years, but you kept your word.*
- *It's true. You had accepted with the condition that I get closer to Kevin.*
- *Yes. You know very well that my death is not the true reason of his distance. The events may lead one to believe so but it had nothing to do with it.*
- *I know. I had to learn what it was to be humble and I was rudely put to the test by this gesture.*
- *You have done very well John.*
- *But…tell me why…*
- *Why I used my physical death to guide you?*
- *Exactly.*
- *I could have chosen a less severe way, but…*
- *You sure don't fool around with choosing a way…*

John and Mary laugh heartedly.

- *No, you see, if you were able to make it through such a humanly difficult challenge, then you have proven to be quite humble. You could not fake any of it.*
- *You have always known how to handle me.*
- *As proud as you are, I could not take this mission lightly.*
- *Mary...*
- *Yes John.*
- *I miss you so much.*
- *But I'm with you John; I'm always with you.*
- *You know what I mean.*
- *But John, you must also learn about this.*
- *Never the less, it's only human.*
- *Humans are quite week John, you know this very well. Envy, jealousy, and misery...they are also human. But, I'm sure you wouldn't want to remain so human.*
- *No, I know what you're saying but it's so good.*
- *The animals also like it John.*
- *But Mary...in the old days you also...*
- *In the old days, John, it was yesterday.*
- *It has been ten years.*
- *For myself, it was yesterday.*
- *But here...you...we don't make...*
- *No, we do not make love John. We live in love, it's much better. It's divinely better. It's not at all human, it's divine.*
- *There, I don't follow you Mary. How can it be better when it was so good with you Mary?*

Mary gently smiles and indicates John to cease speaking. He becomes quite worried. She then slowly gets up form her seat and John notices her becoming quite radiant. She only has her soft face showing and the remainder of her body becomes as luminous as the light found at the center of the table.

John observes this and is overwhelmed by such beauty. Suddenly Mary surrounds him with her rays, which cause John to feel a tremendous inner peace, and his entire body is filled with deep calming warmth. He closes his eyes and lets himself be carried away with what he is presently living.

He begins laughing and it only gets louder. Still without moving his lips, he declares his deep unconditional love for Mary. She returns these feelings. She controls this entire scene and carries John into her whirlwind of energy. John feels loved as he has never felt before in his life. He feels as light as a feather and reaches an extreme level of blissfulness. Mary literally wraps him and appears to be dancing to such a harmonious music. John attempts to move but fails. He finds himself paralyzed by this strong courant. He wants to do something more but is quite pleased with simply savoring these intoxicating feelings that he decides to remain still and to take advantage of it all.

Then, slowly, the tension returns to normal and John finds himself seated, once again,in front of Mary.

- *Wow…what was that?*
- *That…it's to live in love John.*
- *It's magnificent, it's wonderful, it's…divine.*
- *Of course it's divine John.*
- *But…why is it that we don't do it like this on earth…*
- *It may be possible but not at this moment…*
- *But why?*
- *It's…how would I put it…non-physical and even less intellectual.*
- *Then we would have to be…poor of spirit to be able to live it.*
- *That's one way of seeing it. A friend of mine, here, told you not so long ago, "Happy are the poor in spirit, heaven is yours" but you did not listen or simply you just did not understand it. You interpreted everything too rationally.*
- *You mean…*

- *Jesus, as we call him. Yes,…he's here.*
- *But Mary…that was almost two thousand years ago.*
- *It was yesterday John.*
- *But what exactly did he mean?*
- *One day you will understand John.*

Suddenly, John feels the wind picking up. A certain freshness wraps him. He looks around in an attempt to figure out what is happening to him and turns towards Mary but she is already gone. Slowly, the sky becomes darks and then lightening begins. A rumble of thunder tremendously shakes the ground beneath John's feet and instantly he closes his eyes, certain he's to be hit by it.

That is where John wakens. Outside, it is raining "cats and dogs". Rain in December…it has been seen before but it was quite irregular to have thunder and lightening with it.

John remains stretched out on the couch and appears to be waking up calmly in spite of this unexpected storm.

He grabs his latest manuscript and notes a few things, then, puts his pen down and begins talking to himself.

- *Thank you Mary, it was fantastic. I know you're here, I love you, you know. I will never make love again, I will live in love. Thank you Mary.*

John gets up and heads for his warm and inviting bed as the rain ceases outside. He notices this coincidence and a few minutes later, as he was unable to fall asleep, he looks outside and observes white fluffy snowflakes falling gently. John smiles and as he turns around to once again head to his bed, says to himself:

- *You are so terrible.*

To these words, John manages to fall asleep once again. He goes through a few quiet hours before he begins to dream again.

This time, he is on a more familiar terrain. He sees himself in a ski resort accompanied by Simeon. They are waiting in line for the chair lift where several persons are taking it, in turn.

This mountain has something quite particular. It has several levels and one can descend the lift at the level he chooses.

Before their turn arrives, a man with long white hair and a peaceful look, hands two sticks to John.

- *Here my brave Sir, you will need these for the second phase.*

Mechanically, John takes the sticks without questioning their use and takes his place with Simeon on the lift.

Arrived at the first level Simeon informs John that he wishes to not go any further but John attempts to retain him. Nonetheless, Simeon insists and John has no option but to let him go.

- *Stay with me John.* Yells out Simeon.
- *No, I can't. I must make my way to the next step. Go ahead, you'll see, it's not that bad.*
- *John, I'm scared to go alone, I could fall.*
- *Don't worry, there will always be someone near you. And also, I'll always be there. You only have to think of me and I'll come and give you a hand. You'll make it, I'm sure.*
- *But you, where are you going?*
- *I don't know yet. All I know is that it's the second phase.*

As the chair lift begins to move up again, Simeon yells to John to throw him his bag containing all his personal belongings, which he had forgotten on the lift. The lift continues to move up and John is further and further away. Finally John turns to Simeon and says.

- *Never mind Simeon, you won't need it anymore.*

John disappears up the mountain and Simeon finds himself surrounded by strangers who appear sympathetic.

On the other hand, John arrives at the second phase and recognizes someone who he has ignored for quite some time. It consists of his sister Solenne.

John and Solenne had grown up in the same family but had never really gotten to know each other.

- *I didn't know that you could ski Solenne.*
- *Come on, it's been quite some time that I have quit skiing.*
- *But, what are you doing here then?*
- *I was waiting for you. You took quite a long time.*
- *I…*

John is not sure what Solenne is trying to tell him.

- *Come, let's leave hear. We still have plenty to do.*
- *But what?*
- *We have to give a conference on a mountain.*

Being that dreams don't have the same sense of meanings, John accepts and follows Solenne.

Suddenly, they find themselves in a construction site.

- *What are we doing here, I'm completely lost.* Says John.

- *Don't worry. It's going to hurt. We're going to work like you've never worked before. The rule of the game is to get out of it with as few injuries possible but to get out of it.*
- *You call that a game!*

They were surrounded by threats. Enormous trucks attempted to make them deviate from their route, certain walls fell on them to make them back up, but in no circumstance were they to back up, otherwise they would be lost.

Solenne appeared to know what was happening and every time John reacted to a threat she encouraged him to confront it and to not back up or deviate from his route.

- *Use your powers.* Solenne repeatedly told John.
- *But what dam powers. You haven't seen this guy, he measures over three meters and he's coming straight at me with an enormous club.*
- *You can beat him... Don't let him get you. You will encounter many more like him. They don't want you to succeed.*
- *Succeed what? I don't even know what I'm doing here.*
- *Advance, it's too late to go back. I'll explain as we go along. You wanted to skip some levels, well now you have to act and then you will understand.*

John lived several challenges and every time he felt like quitting, a single word from Solenne made him resist.

A short while later, they were almost finished in crossing the construction site, only a lake remained.

- *Did you see this lake; it smells so awful you want to vomit. I suppose I have to swim across? Of course, it's also filled with all kinds of garbage…it's so disgusting.*
- *And why not?*

- *No, but do you have a problem in your head or what?!*

Solenne pushes him and without realizing it, John dives in. Soon after, he finds himself out of the lake, exhausted but happy.

Solenne and John are suddenly transported in a big school, alone in one classroom, and are talking.

- *Was that the second phase? Asks John.*
- *Yes, that's it.*
- *It's a good thing you were there, otherwise…*
- *I had no choice but to come and get you. I was informed that you were coming…quite rapidly I might add. I was told that otherwise, you would get lost.*
- *Tell me about it! I would have been better off grabbing Simeon's bag and joining him.*
- *You would have lost a lot of time but since you were determined to go further, I believed it was worth it.*
- *But you, where did you make it?*
- *It's not important. Let's take a little brake and then we'll continue.*
- *Oh, by the way, what's the story with the two sticks,…I didn't even use them. I even wonder where they are. With all this commotion I believe I have lost them.*
- *Hopefully. That's the secret. One must not use them but loose them.*

John begins laughing tremendously.

- *No, but what's the problem?! I receive something that I must absolutely loose.*
- *That's it.*
- *But…what did I loose.*
- *Probably what you had to loose.*
- *But…I don't follow.*

- *Come on; get up, you'll know soon enough.*

John gets up and observes Solenne leave.

- *Hey Solenne, where are you going? And me, where do I go?*
- *We'll meet up again later.*

John turns around and feels sucked in by a tremendous force. This gets faster and everything around him blackens. He lets himself be carried by the courant without any worries, as if this were normal and expected.

John wakes up abruptly. He feels his heart pounding and has trouble breathing. In less than two minutes he gets hold of his senses and as a tradition, makes notes in his manuscript.

John looks at the time. It is three in the morning. He wraps himself in his blankets as though he had just completed a harsh task and quietly drifts off, in a sleep…without dreams.

Seventh Chapter

When morning arrived John knew very well what he had to do. Not only did he know it, he also felt it. It was a must that he call his sister Solenne whom he had not spoken to for over twenty years.

It is not that he didn't like her but their age difference of six years just did not bring them close.

At age sixteen Solenne left home to continue her studies out of town which brought them to see each other only during Christmas holidays or briefly during summer brakes.

Later on, at the age of eleven, John also left home for his studies which rendered their encounters even more rare.

At the end of her studies Solenne moved to the United States and at that point, his sister basically became an acquaintance.

John had always somewhat envied his sister, observing that she always managed to succeed with ease. Her school grades always impressed the teachers and John found that following his sister's steps while trying to do as well was a heavy load to bear. Knowing that she was so far away helped ease these feelings.

Furthermore, John always believed that his sister would respect him only if he accomplished something valuable in life. This is what brought him to politics. Lead by his pride, he wanted to impress her.

But, that morning, John understood that he had to re-establish contact with Solenne. No matter what her reaction would me, he had to go through with it.

Something was going to happen but like every time prior, John was unable to guess what exactly did the images in his dream signify.

John was caught deep in his thoughts when the phone rang. He glances at the time; eight o'clock.

- *Who in the world would be calling at this hour? He mumbles.*

This was bound to surprise John because it was an extremely rare thing for his phone to ring. Very few people ever called him. The only ones who did were usually either publicity companies or a polling, but then again, never at this hour.

- *Yes hello, says John in a bothered tone.*
- *John…*

He did not immediately recognize the caller and after hesitating a few seconds, continued;

- *Yes, it's me.*
- *How are you? States the caller.*
- *Not bad at all, thank you…but, who am I speaking with?*
- *Come on John, we spent a good part of our lives together; you could not have*
- *forgotten me.*
- *I'm not quite certain…is it you Solenne?*

At the other end Solenne amuses herself and continues.

- *Of course it's me, your "big sister".*
- *Well what do you know; you'll never believe me.*
- *What about?*
- *No, it's impossible. It's just impossible.*
- *What's wrong John, you're worrying me.*
- *If I had a witness, I'd subpoena him immediately…imagine that I actually dreamt of*
- *you last night and I've taken this habit of writing down my most remarkable dreams…. I actually noted this one last night.*
- *Oh, yes, stated Solenne attempting to act surprised.*
- *What if I told you that it's been twenty years since we've spoken and the morning after I dream of you, you call me…*
- *Don't you find that weird John?* Questions Solenne not absolutely certain of whom she really is speaking with.
- *It could be that way for certain people, it could even be called a coincidence, but for myself, it's part of a certain reality.*

John suddenly feels that he is once again revealing himself too quickly and stops.

Solenne then continues.

- *You know John, you are so right. If I'm calling you it is because I have not been able to get you off my mind for the past two weeks. I don't know what's gotten into me but since I could not shake this feeling of wanting to call you I decided to follow my intuition, and so here I am.*
- *But tell me this, it must be quite early in California at this moment?*

- *Yes, It's exactly five in the morning but I did not sleep very well and since I was awake, I figured that instead of just laying in bed I may as well take care of this matter.*

John finds himself laughing out loud.

- *If you knew everything we did last night you would understand why you had trouble sleeping.*
- *Oh yeah?*
- *A crazy dream, absolutely weird but let me tell you that there was a lot of action.*
- *Even I woke up exhausted.*

Then, John and Solenne reminisce their life stories of the past twenty years to bring each other up to the present time.

- *And yourself,* continues John, *are you still with that good old Frank?*
- *Oh no, actually, that story is presently coming to an end.*
- *Don't tell me…*
- *And yes, we spent part of our lives together but the time has come for us to go our separate ways.*
- *You appear to be taking this with a lot of wisdom*
- *Yes…*answers Solenne on a disenchanted tone.
- *Holy God, you appear to talk about it as though it were a completed task.*
- *Bof…it's almost that.*

At this moment the discussion between the two takes a very philosophical tone and they discover each other.

Solenne appears satisfied to see everything that John could have stored as lessons learned from his experiences and John rejoices in realizing that he is not alone in his new way of thinking.

This conversation lasted way over an hour but John finally reroutes it back to Solenne's divorce.

- *So, I guess you are now taking a second chance in life.*
- *Yes, or I would probably replace it with the fact that I'm now contin-uing where I left off, twenty years ago.*
- *Don't tell me that you have been living like a vegetable for all those years.*
- *No, of course not. I've had a good and easy life but on the evolutional level I've been dragging behind, but now I feel I have a part to do. It's as though I've been on stand-by for all these years.*
- *You know what Solenne, here life may appear very long to us but in reality it's only a short learning period.*
- *I know…I know and that is why I believe I must do what I have to. Nothing was progressing. Him, he's now living in a rational and financial world without thinking for a moment that there is more to life where as I'm trying to find where I come from and where I'm going.*
- *Yeah, I understand. It's not easy to communicate, we quickly find ourselves alone, I know very well what it is you mean.*
- *It must be the price to pay,* states Solenne in a tone of abandonment.
- *And how is he taking this?*
- *Oh well, he says that I'm exhausted, that I'm having a burn-out or maybe just home sick…he doesn't really understand.*
- *He cannot understand Solenne.*
- *I know but I still have to make him accept it.*
- *Talk his language, he'll understand better.*
- *What do you mean…?*
- *Well tell him…tell him, for example, that there is nothing left between you, that you don't love him anymore, that you don't feel close to him…I don't know, but do you see what I mean.*

- *Oh, I've said it all, I've done it all but he's stuck on the idea of "professional fatigue" as one of his medical friends would put it. He even wanted me to see a shrink, can you imagine?*
- *Yeah, quite the crowd they are…*
- *The worst part is that to obtain a quick divorce there are only three reason's one can state: adultery, physical or mental abuse.*
- *Not easy to choose.*
- *No…he does not hit me, does not harass me and did not cheat on me, at least not that I'm aware of. As for me, I don't see myself beating him up and I believe I've had enough sex that now I feel too relieved to give in to it by obligation.*
- *So, you are presently separated?*
- *Yes, that's it. We have to wait a year for the divorce to be final.*
- *Luckily, it's easier these days. Do you realize that our parents and their parents had to live in those situations until one of them died?*
- *That's the way it was John. It had to be that way; otherwise we would not be here today. That forced people to get along and to improve certain aspects of their character bringing them to evolve in a certain way. It was done as a religious, moral or social obligation but at the end of it all, they evolved in a certain way.*
- *This actually brought different scenarios depending on the person but absolutely everyone was influenced by the imposed rules. Today…they no longer have their reason for being!*
- *But, today, people must still evolve; therefore, shouldn't we enforce the ties of marriage Solenne?*
- *Not at all, marriage is an institution of the past. People, as you put it, are becoming more and more aware of their needs to evolve and not being obliged to be in wedlock to do so. But also, marriage remains an option for those who need it, for those who, without its guidance would go wrong!*
- *But the bible…*
- *What about the bible?*

- *It states that we unite with each other 'til death do us part...*
- *What death would that be John, do you know?*
- *I see where you are coming from...there is a sense of order in your reasoning.*
- *It's easy to reason when we have well understood the true meaning of things.*
- *There, you are teaching me something new Solenne. Continue, I'm quite interested.*
- *Well, here I go. I know that you can reply that there are many different types of religion and several models of society. They may run differently but the notion of couples or union exists in all of them and the institution of marriage, had some form or another in all the societies. Depending on the level of evolution of each individual, he/she will be born in such or such a type of society which will best meet his needs for evolving.*
- *What you are saying is that all the social traditions and all the religions are valuable and that they also have their reason for being...*
- *Of course, they are only a guide, protection in some sort. Nobody is right, basically, everyone is wrong. Each and everyone has chosen or was imposed the life that serves him best.*
- *But there exists such great differences, Solenne.*
- *That goes in hand with the differences that may exist between such and such a person, or such and such a population. Each is not at the same level of evolution. But, more and more these differences disappear, which explains why the migrating inter-racial movements are more and more numerous. The walls are slowly falling, actually, they must fall! We will build the tower of Babel...but backwards.*
- *But if it is so...*

John becomes very pensive and appears to have come upon a revelation which renders him mysterious and worried.

- *John…are you still there?*
- *But of course…that's it, that really is it!! Do you realize what you have just told me*
- *Solenne?*
- *I think so but go ahead, I'm all ears.*
- *When a couple has reached its maturity, or if you prefer, when the fact of living together prevents one or the other, or both, to continue one's path, the next step is separation so that one can continue his way at his own speed, each having reached a different level of evolu-tion, having used the other as an evolutional tool. As though we were going to re-incarnate in another couple, towards new experiences which we need to survive. Isn't that what you mean?*
- *That's correct. We could be at the same level today but be kilometers apart in five, ten or fifteen years. The opposite is also true. We could be very distant today and find ourselves face to face in two or ten years. This depends on the speed in which each evolves. Just as two people may follow each other on the evolution plan and live an entire lifetime together without feeling any effects or by being withheld by the other, it's what we call combined mutual evolution. Each sup-ports the other and each participates in the growth of the other. Unfortunately, this is extremely rare and will be so more and more. It is good to have distance but when it becomes too pronounced, con-tact does not occur anymore. You're right, separation must take place, for the well being of both parties. And, instead of declaring war we should simply say; "Thank-you for all that you have given me" period. The worst would be to do as our predecessors and spend the rest of our lives playing victim or the misunderstood. What a waste of precious time. At the extreme, each would become independent and self-sufficient.*
- *But what about the children in all that…?*
- *The children follow our examples in all of it. Let's give them the good so that they*

- *don't have to spend a life learning simple insignificant things. Children don't have the necessary tools to confront such situations and when we also have them believe that a union is forever and then one day you impose a separation which they did not expect, it is clear that the shock will confuse them. It's as though you have said; "Everything we have been teaching you is no longer true, we are changing the rules this morning, sometimes separation is better". How do you expect them to understand? It's up to us to understand the proper things and to teach it to them... in advance.*
- *But children need their parents.*
- *They especially need mature parents who live in harmony, together or not! Children are often a link between two persons who needed this link to re-enforce their spiritual inter-relationship. On the other hand, we have a role to play in their evolution but neither the children nor the parent must slow down the other in this multiple inter-relationship. You see, finally, it's so simple.*
- *And we so easily complicate everything...*
- *Yeah, maybe one day. One day we'll understand it all!*
- *But let's take it further. Let's do the parallel of this with society and religions. Can't you see the logical explanation to the disappearance of certain antic populations? To the extinction of certain societies? Can't you also see that certain societies and religions are called upon to disappear if they do not follow this flow of evolution?*
- *It's inevitable John, but the worst of it is that this is to be done with pain and controversy where these people and/or religions could actually disappear to give way to new structures without hassle or pain. It would only take that we understand that such or such a religion or society is outdated and decide to create a new one better suited for present realities, as a couple who separated to form a new union with another person. Unfortunately, mankind has become too attached to his little world. By adapting to the changes we would modify it*

beyond recognition, almost as if it had…disappeared…to give way to others, better and greater.

- *To evolve with pain…are you talking about the wars and cataclysms?*
- *Yes. We cannot delay the movement of evolution and all these great forces of nature are somewhat necessary when man has not moved forward on his own.*
- *Are you trying to tell me that Hitler and Napoleon, or as the atomic bomb on Hiroshima and Nagasaki were necessary?*
- *Hitler was nothing but a miserable puppet. His work, as horrible as it was, could have been prevented if we had understood certain things at that time. Same thing for Hiroshima, Napoleon, etc…You can go as far back as the crucifixion of Christ if you want, each and every time someone said "Forgive them Father, they do not know what they are doing".*
- *We prefer to understand after the fact. We react, only react, simply react…it's disgusting! Therefore, it is not just that it is necessary but…it's quickly becoming…. inevitable!!*
- *Wow…you really floored me with that!*
- *It is so true John. But, go try and yell this on the church steps tomorrow morning. They will lock you up just as they used to burn those who possessed some lucidity and could predict the future in the olden days.*
- *But should we believe that century after century mankind commits the same errors, over and over again?*
- *Unfortunately, and the means in their powers get stronger and it only goes from bad to worst.*
- *The third world war, predicted by Nostradamus for 1999, would therefore be inevitable?*
- *The way things are going now…I'd believe so. But, mankind always has the possibility to react!*
- *Do you believe that the infamous people of Atlantis, if it really did exist, disappeared because of its stubbornness?*
- *It's either that or they crossed a frontier which we are still looking for.*

- *Let's go back to Nostradamus. It is said that only forty to fifty percent of his predictions have proven to be true.*
- *So we managed to bypass a few. Did we actually act in view of bypassing them or is it the billiard effect, we'll never know.*
- *Did you say the "billiard effect"?*
- *Yes…that's something else. Quickly…you know how to play pool?*
- *Yes, I love it.*
- *Therefore, you know very well that a slight difference in your angle and in the force used to project your ball will modify the course of the game. Try this…mark all the balls on a billiard's table by using a chalk and marking the spot where they are on the table. Play your ball attempting to succeed it properly. Afterwards, notice the position of each ball.*
- *Then, replace all the balls on their original spots, which you had marked and try again but modify your aim by about one degree and your force used. Afterwards, notice the new position of the balls. You will observe that on your second attempt you found yourself facing an entirely different game. It's exactly like that with every shot. This is what the billiard's effect is all about. The rest of the game depends entirely on your present shot.*
- *A single change in orientation is of nature to provoke or avoid a war…*
- *That's correct. Also, it doesn't take much today to create an insurmountable catastrophe in two or ten years just as it takes very little to provoke a series of events to bring us to accomplish another wonder. A few degrees, a little more or less force, "that's all it takes"!*

- *Yeah…I'm learning so much from you, it's unreal! If we push reasoning to its limit, when everyone will have understood all this and will have reached the same level, there shouldn't be any more wars, or boundaries, or different cultures, or different religions…there will only be…*

- *…But one world. It will be the end of the world as we know it presently, and that will be for the best! There will be universal peace, three thousand years of peace, without pain, without misery, without poverty, just as Nostradamus predicts.*
- *Where will we be then?*
- *Definitely not here…I believe that is why Nostradamus was unable to see anything more after those three thousand years.*
- *But afterwards?*
- *Afterwards it will be up to another specie to take the place. We will become part, as the people of Atlantis, of a specie that completely disappeared from the surface of the earth and the new "owners" of the planet will throw themselves, as we did, in the research of answering why we disappeared, etc etc…They will follow our traces as we follow those of our predecessors.*
- *But them, where are they at, our predecessors,…those whom we say are much more evolved than us?*
- *They are where we will be next. I already told you. We are following them. We will continue on another planet, we will have crossed the barrier of time, in another galaxy or something of the sort…how am I suppose to know?!*
- *We will have another one, made differently and in accordance to our new needs. Will it be physical or not…Impossible to know at the moment.*
- *Therefore, the earth is some sort of giant laboratory where we are realizing our own experiments?*
- *In some sort, yes.*

John becomes quiet and takes a moment of silence before continuing.

- *And I thought I knew it all…*
- *Oh boy! There is still so much more but what good is it…we have to wait for the others. I'm just here waiting.*

- *You believe that...*
- *Yes...I believe that some of us are ready to cross over. Some have already done it. But we cannot choose to go ourselves.*
- *What do you mean exactly?*
- *Well, what if I told you that on certain days I would gladly take my one-way ticket out of here?!*
- *You're thinking of...*
- *Death, yes, but we call that "suicide" and that is strictly forbidden. It's extremely lazy and selfish.*
- *Selfish you say?*
- *Yes, it's selfish because it is as though you quit fighting and advancing, to work on yourself for the common good and if you give up today and you return in a hundred years, you will start over where you left off. Also, since society will have continued evolving without you, you will have to work twice as hard the next time. It's also selfish because even if you have reached a superior level, you must remain to help others as you have been helped.*
- *How can we know if we have reached the door to cross over to the other world?*
- *You will feel it. But, the manner in which you are presently speaking john, I believe you are almost there.*
- *But besides the two of us, do you believe there is anyone else there yet?*
- *There are plenty. Fortunately there are more and more but the time has not yet come for us to meet. We are all somewhat alone with our dreams...certain of them discretely let us know but it is up to us to recognize them, they won't approach us.*
- *Who exactly are you talking about?*
- *Prophets, in some sort...modern prophets, as was pronounced in the bible.*
- *Where...who?*
- *We see them everywhere John and we hear them everywhere.*

- *I don't have a clue who you are talking about. I sure hope you don't mean these pathetic so called preachers who are still attempting to have us swallow all the passages of the bible...*
- *No. I'm talking about the artists, singers, musicians, poets, film producers and writers. They are our modern prophets.*
- *What about the politicians?*
- *Bof...unfortunately, they are simple puppets but are still somewhat useful. They are nothing but instruments. Just as are doctors, lawyers, psychiatrists etc. They are still very useful but one day their mandate will be complete, then they will have to recycle themselves.*
- *I see...I understand. The messages are poring on us but we are unable to decipher them.*
- *That's it. We could rewrite the bible and we would still completely misinterpret it.*
- *So they are all prophets then...*
- *Yes, but beware of the falsified copies. There are several. The most popular are not necessarily the real ones.*
- *Therefore, the real prophets have not yet been recognized?*
- *Oh, yes, some of them have. For example, take John Lennon. He was a true prophet. Listen to his song "IMAGINE", everything is in it, from the beginning to the end. He clearly states, "I hope some day you'll join us". What do you think he was talking about? He came to deliver his message of love to then return where he came from in hopes that we do join him some day.*
- *The bible even warns us that several prophets will come before the return of Christ and that some of them would be fake. You only have to look around yourself; it's clear to see. We end up being able to feel who is white and who is black.*
- *And Christ...is he really going to return?*
- *John...you're not seriously asking me this question are you?*

John glances at the time, it's ten o'clock.

- *Listen Solenne, I would gladly talk with you all day. I have the impression that I have a lot of catching up to do. I must also be at the doctors by eleven, some discomfort I've been dragging along.*
- *Nothing serious I hope?*
- *No, just some slight pain in my back, that's all. But I just want to reassure myself.*
- *Anyways, I have to get up soon. I have to meet with someone…I should introduce him to you some day.*
- *Hey listen, why don't you come over this summer?*
- *Oh, I don't know, I'd like to but I have so much to take care of with this divorce…why don't you come over?*
- *I'd love to but my poor Candy is so tired.* Says John jokingly.

Solenne had forgotten that John had just informed her that he was living on a modest budget.

- *Ok, well, in any case, I'll call you back.*
- *That's it…let's keep in touch.*

John hangs up the phone and releases a sigh of satisfaction.

- *Wow! I'll have to write all of this down when I return.*

Eighth Chapter

Spring finally arrived. The trees slowly awoke and showed signs of rebirth.

The sun grew in strength and melted away the last signs of snow on the ground.

Around John's home, birds began building their nests for the warm season coming up.

John had spent the remainder of the winter season working on his notes and his phone calls with Solenne multiplied up to two or three a week.

Each and every time they spoke the conversations lasted for quite some time. They never lasted less than an hour.

As every morning, the "journalist" delivers the paper and honks. Not so long ago Victor, the journalist would depart without further delay but for the past few months he made it a point to exchange a few words with John who, slowly, had regained sympathy from the entire village.

- *How is it going this morning John?*
- *Not bad at all. Did you see this marvelous day Victor?*

- *And I believe that I'm going to improve on this magnificent day of yours.*

Victor hands John his newspaper and a letter.

- *It comes from the United States.* Says Victor.
- *I'll be dam…I have a feeling I know who it comes from.*
- *Let me know if it's the president.*

Victor starts the engine of his vehicle and salutes John, who returns this gesture.

John quickly sits on his porch steps and anxiously opens the envelope.

- *I can't believe this, I just can't believe it.* Exclaims John as he observes its contents.

John stairs at the papers with great joy.

- *It's unbelievable. I could have never hoped for this.*

He had just received a plane ticket for Los Angeles. Solenne absolutely wanted to meet with John and since she could not leave LA and since she knew very well that John could not afford to pay his trip there, she simply decided to send him this ticket. It did not take much time for John to run to the phone in order to thank his sister.

At the other end Solenne answers in a very low and faint tone of voice.

- *Hello…*
- *Solenne…It's John. I've just received your letter.*

Solenne figures that John did not take the time to verify the hour it was and attempts to make him feel uncomfortable.

- *Hey, by the way…do you know what time it is here?*

Having been caught up in the play, John becomes uneasy and does not quite know how to find a way out of it.

- *Eeee, it's true, I hadn't…*

Solenne immediately interrupts John in fear that he may take it seriously.

- *It's all right little brother, I was just pulling your leg.*

Uncertain, John continues on the same tone.

- *I can call back later you know.*
- *No, no. I always get up quite early and it's very rare that I wake up later than six*
- *o'clock. It gives me a complete hour to welcome the day and relax a little before entering our sad terrestrial reality. So, you finally received it?*
- *You did not have to do this but…I gladly accept it.*
- *It took some time to get there. Did you check the departure date not to miss anything?*
- *Well, actually, that is why I'm calling you now; I have to leave tonight at eight.*
- *Oh…a bit longer and it wouldn't have worked but I had taken insurance.*
- *It doesn't give me much time but I have very little to settle before leaving. I'm not*
- *attached to anything here besides my sweet Candy whom I will leave to Simeon for caring.*
- *In any case, I'm real anxious to see you John. I'll pick you up at the airport tonight.*

- *You should be arriving in the early morning hours but I'll be there, you can count on it.*
- *Okay, so, see you later, I've got to go pack and I'm on my way.*

John hangs up the phone and remains there, staring, for a few seconds.

- *Oh boy.. Here we go.* He says proudly.

John immediately heads for the stables and chats a little with Candy while he prepares her harness.

- *Your old John is going away for a few days but you'll be in good hands and besides,*
- *the place where I'm bringing you has a bunch of animals much less boring then I. You'll see, it's a five star hotel for horses. You deserve it after all this time.*

John immediately makes his way to Simeon's house and crosses him as he was heading for the fields with his humungous tractor.

Simeon stops the engine and descends from it to find out what John could possibly want.

- *Hello there little brother.* States John.
- *Quite the early bird my Johnny. What brings you here at such an hour?*
- *I really won't be long Simeon. I'm leaving this evening for California.*
- *Wow, you don't go out much but when you do…*
- *It's Solenne.* Interrupts John.
- *What, is something wrong?*
- *On the contrary. You remember last winter when I told you that she and I spoke*
- *often? Well, she invited me over and I must be at the airport tonight. She invited me.*

- *Too bad that you're going. Must I conclude that you want me to store this "baggage"*
- *of yours?*
- *Yeah, if you don't mind.*
- *Don't worry about it; you know how I love animals. If anyone touches her he will be*
- *eating his eyebrows with his upper teeth.*

Simeon takes Candy's harness and begins softly talking to her.

- *You'll see my dear; we'll make you a very comfortable place here. Afterwards, you*
- *won't even want to go back home. Actually, there is a large stall that was freed yesterday. We just put fresh hay; it's a paradise for an old mare as yourself.*

Simeon guides Candy to the stables and then returns to John.

- *Give me two minutes and I'll give you a lift back to your place.*

John has no choice but to accept and expresses his content.

Once arrived at his home, John salutes Simeon and in a hurry, enters the house.

Simeon stick his head out the car window and yells to John;

- *I'll pick you up at three; we'll be at the airport by six, okay?*

Overwhelmed by the rapid events of his day, John, through a window, gestures that he accepts by giving Simeon a hand salute.

Precisely three o'clock and Simeon is on time. John exits his home carrying a handbag and a suitcase that appears to be extremely heavy.

- *What in God's name did you pack in here?* Questions Simeon as he places the suitcase in the car trunk.
- *Oh, I brought my books.*
- *I sure hope you don't plan on just sitting around reading while you're in California.*
- *No, it's Solenne who wishes to have a look at them.*

Simeon remains baffled.

- *What about your clothes?*
- *Oh, they're in here.* States John indicating his handbag.
- *Ok…each his own choice.*

And so, without further delay, they get in the vehicle and depart for Montreal.

On their way to the airport, John and Simeon discussed John and Solenne's new situation. During this talk Simeon attempts to get closer to John and confesses;

- *You know John, I believe that you have your head on straight and I'm certain that you*
- *are right. I didn't read all the books you did and I didn't understand everything you tried to tell me but I know one thing, since you have told me about life, our role hear etc…I see things much differently.*
- *What do you mean, exactly?*
- *I don't quite know how to tell you this but…it's as though I don't see life in the same*
- *way anymore. It's as though I feel myself taking another direction.*
- *In what way?*

- *How would I put it…you know, it was important for me to succeed, to own land, nice*
- *buildings and all the rest. Now, it's as if all that was not important anymore. It's not that I believe it's wrong to have all of it but I no longer think it's necessary.*
- *It was for you Simeon.*
- *Yes, but not anymore. I'm quite happy to have all of it but should I lose it, it would be*
- *easier to accept, much easier.*
- *And why is that?*
- *Because…because if I lose it, it's probably because I no longer need it…*

John gives Simeon a very satisfied look. Afterwards, Simeon continues;

- *There we go, it's gotten to the point where I'm now talking like you.*
- *Don't worry; it's not a disease.* Says John laughing.
- *Want to know something else…there was a time when I was afraid to lose everything and I would work form sun up to sun down to consolidate my profits but now, I work…simply to kill time and through my work I'm learning and observing many things that I had never noticed before.*
- *And how do you feel?*
- *Free, liberated, detached in some way. I'm living!*
- *Detachment…that's it. It's the first step.*
- *The first step?* Questions Simeon.
- *Yes, but let's not go there. One day you will understand.*

This was followed by a long period of silence where both brothers were content in gazing at the road. Afterwards, at approximately ten minutes way from the airport, John resumed the conversation.

- *You know Simeon, I didn't really tell you anything. I barely scratched the surface on*
- *the subject. I could give you a twenty-four hour monologue without repeating the same thing twice and I still would not have covered one-hundredth of it.*
- *But what could be so important John?*

John remained silent for a moment and continued.

- *Why don't you come with me? Take the plane in two days and come join me.*

Simeon becomes quite uncomfortable and replies.

- *I don't believe that would be such a good idea.*
- *Why not? You could learn a lot. Solenne is much more advanced then I. Actually,*
- *I'm not going there to teach her anything, on the contrary, I'm going there to learn.*

Simeon keeps his position and refuses.

- *In any case John, I think it would be too much for me. I feel it, that's all. I have the*
- *impression I'm just starting to learn how to walk and what you are asking me is to go and run a marathon. Honestly, I don't feel ready.*

John acknowledges and concludes.

- *You're completely right Simeon. You cannot order this and to try and go too fast*

- *could be bad.*

Simeon feels somewhat humiliated for having confided so much and takes a deep breath while stopping the vehicle in front of the "departing" entrance of the airport.

Both men get out of the vehicle and Simeon hands John his heavy suitcase.

This scene becomes emotional when both brothers approach each other but don't quite know how to bid farewell.

Simeon makes the first move.

- *Do you want to know what I'm thinking about John?*
- *Yes Simeon, go ahead, I'm listening.*

With a voice filled with emotions, Simeon continues.

- *Ten years ago, I lost you and believed you had hit rock bottom, to be exact. I thought I had lost you forever. But, six months ago when I found you, I felt very happy. I had just found my big brother with whom I had had such joy. And then, today…I…I feel as though I'm losing you again. I believe you have moved very fast John and that you have reached a level where I can no longer reach you.*

John sheds a tear and reassures Simeon.

- *Simeon, you are my favorite brother. I will always be your brother and even if our ideas are distant, I'll remain close to you, forever. I will never abandon you again Simeon*
- *You only said that to make me fell better but I can very well feel that we are losing each other again John.*

John does not really know what to answer anymore.

- *Don't worry Simeon; believe me…some day, yes, one day we will be together forever.*
- *I must go now Simeon.*

Then John holds Simeon in his arms and Simeon sniffles back his tears, unable to hide his emotions. The embrace lasts a few seconds and both brothers finally let go and mutually wish each other " bon voyage".

John enters the airport and immediately makes his way to the registration desk.

Two hours later the plane takes off and John realizes that Solenne did not spare a thing. He is seated in first class and takes advantage of all the comfort which comes with this privilege.

The flight lasts a good five hours and John accepts the meal that he is served to then let himself be carried off by his daydreaming. He looks out his window and observes angel silhouettes within the carpet of clouds. He attempts to show interest to what is taking place within the aircraft but nothing grabs his attention.

Tired, cradled by the engine noise and cuddled by the comfort of his seat, John can no longer resist and is carried off into his sleep.

Ninth Chapter

John gets up, straight as a board, just as we would erect a prefabricated wall. And so, he now finds himself standing, in the aircraft and begins to look around.

He sees his body, just in front of himself, comfortably relaxed in his seat. In spite this irregular situation, John does not feel worried.

Everything he sees is identical to reality; the members of the crew moving about, the color of the seats, the passengers, he even very clearly hears the conversations, even those furthest from his position.

John appears aware of his state. He realizes very well that he is there, standing, in the center of the alley, but that nobody appears to have noticed his presence there.

An elderly lady, who is seated nearby, appears very concentrated in her reading and John attempts to speak with her.

- *Excuse me mam; do you know where the bathroom is?*

The lady does answer him and does not even appear to have been disturbed in any way. John presumes she may be hard of hearing and attempts again but this time lays his hand on her shoulder.

- *Excuse me mam…*

The lady mechanically replaces her shawl she had on her shoulders and turns towards her husband, seated next to her.

- *Excuse me, did you say something?*
- *No.* Answered the man.
- *I thought…I was caught in my reading.*

John clearly notices that something is not quite right but attempts again, having noticed that the woman reacted.

- *It's me, John Chabot; it is I who is speaking to you…*

But, at this moment, the woman began an unrelated conversation with her husband and nothing further reached her.

John accepts this state of being and decides to venture through the alleys.

He sees everything as real. A young child playing with his toys, this business man crumbling a piece of paper, two lovers, newlyweds which appear attached to each other by the lips, and finally, John arrives, without realizing it, in the small bathroom. It was though all he had to do was think of a place and he would instantly find himself there.

In the bathroom, a stewardess was busy while staring at the center page of a magazine.

John was dumbfounded.

- *Forgive me miss…I was not aware that it was occupied.*

The young lady does not react and John, embarrassed, leaves the bathroom.

- *Holy gees, I must surely be dreaming.* Says John to himself.

Finally, aware of the privilege he holds, John decides to have some fun with it.

He plays the impertinent while listening to the most intimate conversations, he reviews the notes of a woman working on a project, he attends the kitchen area to tease the stewardesses who are unaware of his presence, he then stops in front of this other woman who is in her forties. He notices that there is a small gray cloud over one of the woman's breasts. This grabs his attentions and John realizes that he has just discovered an important element.

Without further ceremonies, he continues his trip and makes his way, there, where everyone who boards a plane wishes to go; the cockpit.

He observes all the levers, dials, but he especially notices the very relaxed mood of the crew and remains disconcerted with this.

He overhears the pilot discussing with the copilot;

- *I would sure like to get the tall one in thirty-nine-c.*
- *Yeah…and also, she appears to be traveling alone.*
- *It's not for you buddy; you're too young for her.*

Both men tease each other this way and occasionally glances at the commands.

John feels that to spend five hours staring at the same dials may become hallucinating and that a bit of distraction would only be welcomed.

Finally, satisfied of his tour, John leaves the cockpit and amusingly addresses the pilot;

- *Your zipper is down, you poor imbecile.*

The pilot makes an automatic gesture to verify his zipper and close it while continuing his conversation with his copilot.

At this moment John feels sucked in, as he did in his meeting with Mary in the garden except that this time it's much quicker and John feels as though he's losing control.

He rapidly finds himself in his seat and vaguely hears someone addressing him.

The words are barely perceptive, deafening, as though his ears were full of water.

John is quite aware that he is amongst the real world and would like to react but his body does not respond to any of his commands. He feels heavy, very heavy and unable to move.

The stewardess keeps addressing him and eventually the sounds become clear to John.

- *Mr. Chabot…Mr. Chabot, are you okay?*

John would like to answer but is still unable.

- *Would you like to see a doctor sir?* Questions the young lady.

Finally, John succeeds in letting out a few words but it was as though his tongue weighed five pounds.

- *No…thank you…I'm fine.* He manages to say with great difficulty.
- *Please fasten your seatbelt and bring your seat to the up right position, we are*

- *commencing our descent.*

John manages to move but with great difficulty. Eventually, after a few minutes, he regains his full capacities and takes his appropriate position.

The stewardess returns to her post and passes a comment to her coworker.

- *I'm telling you, 1-C sure is hammered. It's unbelievable to be so drunk, he was barely able to speak or move.*
- *We see all kinds here.* States the other.

At his seat, John retook control of his senses and glances around. He is extremely surprised to notice that everything is exactly as in his dream. He leaves his seat to head for the bathrooms and on his way recognizes the elderly woman whom he had spoken to, then the stewardess he came upon in the bathrooms and finally the lady in her forties who had the gray cloud over her left breast.

Somewhat worried with all this strange similarity, John attempts to see other elements he had observed.

When entering the bathroom, John notices the small clock which he had also noticed upon his earlier untimely intrusion in his dream. He immediately notices the time; it is thirty minutes passed midnight. During his dream he had also noticed the time, it had been fifteen minutes passed midnight, as though his dream had followed the chronological order of time!

John returns to his seat and while doing so encounters the stewardess again.

- *You must not leave your seat, Mr Chabot.*
- *Please forgive me, it was something urgent.* Replies John casually.

The stewardess is surprised to see him so calm and in possession of his abilities. John then continues.

- *Tell me miss, by any chance would the pilot be wearing a red tie, blue jacket and black stockings?*

The stewardess becomes numb and nervously answers.

- *That's exact but how…*
- *Well, all pilots wear a red tie and black stockings.* Answers John amusingly.
- *Of course…of course.* Concluded the young lady, quite troubled.

Once the stewardess departed, John attempts to find the explanation to this extra-ordinary event but remains unfathomable.

Upon return to her post, the young stewardess once again confides in her coworker.

- *There is something not quite "right" about that guy. Earlier he was so drunk and now he's sober. And also, he gave me the details of the pilot's socks…*
- *He probably noticed it at the airport.* Answers the other. *I think he really got you!*
- *Of course…that's it. Wise guy huh! I'm going to get him on his way out.*

Once the plane had landed and all the passengers disembarked, John remained in his seat and appeared wanting to savor every second he is living at the moment.

As the last passenger to exit, the stewardess awaits him with an attitude of superiority.

- *Did you enjoy your flight Mr Chabot?*
- *It was extra-ordinary if I might say so.* Replies John mockingly.
- *And tell me Sir…you appear to be very good at guessing games. You could then*
- *probably tell me the color of my panties?*

John smiles and continues.

- *Do you really want to know?*
- *Go on, we've made it this far…* Replies the stewardess with a condescending tone

while her coworkers look on amusingly.

John hesitates but continues again.

- *They are white with tiny red and blue flower prints.*

The young woman blushes instantly. John prepares to exit while holding back his laughter and then stops in the doorway to add.

- *Oh, by the way…I believe you forgot you magazine in the bathroom earlier.*

Completely stunned, but without time to react, the stewardess rushes to the bathroom to recuperate the magazine before any of her coworkers got hold of it and would guess the scene she had been caught up in.

The others observe this circus of events without understanding while John disappears into the crowd of passengers.

After having claimed his large suitcase, John crosses the sentry position and throws himself in Solenne's arms who was also excited to see him.

After the usual salutations and a few exchanges about the flight, John and Solenne find themselves in the car where John anxiously tells Solenne about his latest adventure.

Solenne listens without reacting but while still appearing fascinated,…we could even say happy about this event.

- *It doesn't seem to surprise you.*
- *You have lived an exceptional experience John.*
- *That, I noticed. But it could not have been a dream, it was so real. Everything was*
- *exactly as in real life, what I saw then I also saw when I was awake. Nevertheless, I was sleeping well and wasn't awake either. Then, when I came to my senses, it's almost as though I was paralyzed, I couldn't talk, nor move, nor hear but I had returned to reality.*
- *• I regained by senses in about three minutes and I realized what I had just lived when I saw certain people that I had seen in my dream.*
- *It wasn't a dream John.*
- *If it wasn't a dream or reality…what was it then?*
- *It was another reality.*
- *Another reality…. what do you mean?*
- *You had an out of body experience, a kind of accidental "debodilization".*
- *A what? An out o body experience. It happens to everyone when they're sleeping. It's usually when we are exhausted and where our physical practically completely abandons us.*
- *But I've never heard anyone speak about heir "debodilization", as you put it.*
- *People are not conscious when doing this. They never remember it.*

- *Okay, but why did I remember it then? Everything I told you is true. You should have seen the stewardess's face.*
- *I believe every word you've told me John. People don't usually remember it because when it happens they are not conscious. Their conscious is...tired. Instead we could say that it is an ultra conscious state.*
- *It's so true...I was conscious of my "unconsciousness".*
- *See, it's like dreaming in full consciousness but one must not confuse the conscious*
- *dreaming with out of body experiences.*
- *First of all, what's the difference?*
- *In a conscious dream, you are still living in the world of dreams with its irrational laws, incompatible with our real perceptions. You can act in your dreams and react with it. In the "debodilization" or "out of body" experience, you only act as a spectator to the real world. You are not within the fantastic world of dreams. You cannot change anything that you are seeing; you have no power except maybe a very modest influence.*
- *Like having someone sense you are talking to them?*
- *That's it, but the person won't hear you, she may react but will not observe anything around her, she will blame it on the fruit of her imagination or a hearing hallucination, as would state a charming psychiatrist. It appears that certain fortunetellers can feel these people which travel in this other dimension. Then again we must separate the true from the fictitious ones...*
- *Wow, but how could that happen to me by mistake?*
- *That's easy, the higher your level of evolution, the higher your emotional level goes and at certain levels there exists other realities which become accessible then. And, since you are in the process of reaching this point, you simply experienced one without trying.*
- *So, someone who has not evolved and is a bad person could not be able to experience*
- *this?*

- *That's something else, in this world, it is not as I've been telling you about the different stages of advance lives where those who have not reached a certain degree of evolution may enter. Therefore, in this world, there exists good and not so good. It is said that there are "white" angels like you and I, and "black" angels.*
- *Angels?*
- *Yes, the term is not exactly correct but that is what we call those who are able to travel in such a world as you did.*
- *Because we are also suppose to be able to do this when we want?*
- *Yes. There are techniques but it isn't worth it John. Don't fool around with that.*
- *Leave it to those who are in search of strong sensations. It's sufficient for you to know that it exists and that it is there if you need it to help yourself or someone else.*
- *As if a black angel came to cause trouble in my "turf"?*
- *That's correct. You would only be able to get rid of him by competing on his terrain.*
- *And what if it turns out that the black angel who is harassing me measures twelve feet and weighs 200kg?*
- *I'm sure you've noticed that the physical aspect has no bearing on that level.*
- *It's true, I wasn't even thinking of my physical being. I didn't care weather I measure two or ten feet tall.*
- *In that world, the true strength is that of the soul, the energy of the heart. The astral world is ruled by pure energetic laws.*
- *The astral world?*
- *Yes, you did an excursion into what we call the astral world. It is a world that is parallel to ours but on a more subtle plan, less physical. There, we find all those who do out of body experiences, the deceased who have left the earth and who have not accepted their deaths, those who committed suicide, and the children born and deceased without having been baptized. It's probably what we call "in waiting".*

- *Therefore, I can sleep safely.*
- *Finally, sure. Because all pure souls represents a force so great that no black angel would dare approach it. They are so week in that world. Those that are bad succeed their plays here, on earth, by intimidation, fraud, violence, rape, etc...but in that world they are completely lost. They attempt to act amongst each other or towards those who are week and vulnerable down here.*
- *As I was saying, it is all based upon our energetic forces; they have a very negative energy, very low; therefore they are very week and vulnerable.*

John attempts to understand all of this and to follow his wise sister.

- *But...if what you are saying is true, and trust me it does make sense, all these people who say they can hear voices or see lights...they are not really crazy?*
- *Of course not. They simply don't have any more control over the situation and presently we only freeze their brains and disconnect them from reality with poisonous potions. We must not blame science, it is all we have at the present to help them. This way they become invulnerable to the low astral world since their physical body no longer reacts but have also become dysfunctional in our world. One day, science will associate itself with natural doctrines and will then be able to find less drastic measures that will be much more efficient.*
- *I would never have guessed that emotional or mental conditions could be cured by going to this level.*
- *On the astral level, of course. The medical world is still too stuck on the belief that the human body is composed simply of cells and atoms. We have admitted that there is a mental and emotional plan without; nonetheless, situating them in the human carcass and that is where they are stuck.*

- *Laugh all you want but it is so true what you have just said. A doctor will tell you that you are suffering from emotional imbalance or mental afflictions but he will never succeed in pinpointing it.*
- *Oh, some will succeed in doing so. They blame it all on the brain. "The brain is dysfunctional" "It's all in your head", so they say! That's a good one. Of course the brain is suffering a malfunction during a mental sickness; it is directly related to the mental plan.*
- *But where exactly are these other plans, or levels?*
- *Outside of the body…as a peal envelopes an apple. In the plane, you lived in the astral world. That is why science has not yet identified them, these "plans" are outside the physical body and they, the doctors, only keep looking for answers in the physical meat carcass which is the human body.*
- *How many plans are there?*
- *Six…or seven, I'm not quite certain.*
- *Six plans…and the physical plan, where is that one situated in there?*

Solenne smiles and explains the following.

- *The physical plan is the lowest. It's the last level of being. That is where the dogs and wolves live. Afterwards, there is the emotional plan, and then the mental. These three plans constitute the terrestrial plan of the human being. The other part, its divine part, constitutes the causal plan, the Buddhist plan and finally the athmique plan.*
- *Well I'll be damm,…we sure have a ways to go!*
- *That's true. When we look around and we see all these retards who believe having reached their ultimate level of evolution, it sure is enough to be depressed. Two thousand years to get here. It's astounding! When will we wake up…?*

Then Solenne and John finally arrive at Solenne's residence. It is a large residence situated on a mountaintop from which one can admire the illuminated city below.

John takes his things and while quite satisfied of his trip, is exhausted and politely asks the direction to his room

Solenne shows him to his room and while getting ready to turn in, she, states.

- *Take all the time you want to sleep; we have the entire house to ourselves. The children won't show up either, they are gone in the desert for two weeks, some sort of retreat.*
- *I would have liked to see them; it's been so long.*
- *We'll be better off this way. We have too many things to do and too much to tell each other. Concludes Solenne.*
- *Ok then, good night.*
- *Good night, John.*

Tenth Chapter

That night John had a very strange dream. A dream worthy of the world of dreams with all of its fantasies and somewhat absurd images. He found no immediate significance to this one but later during the day, its true meaning became clear to him.

In this dream John was somewhat of a giant toy, a white guy blown up with helium and wearing a huge smile on his face. He resembled the famous Quebec City winter carnival mascot. It could also very be similar to the white cartoon character that appears in the Michelin tire commercials on television.

Therefore, John was this huge guy, joyful and gigantic who toured along the shorelines of Los Angeles. He could recognize the half moon shape of this ridge which, of course he had not yet visited in his conscience state.

He must have measured over 100 meters because he could see the city as we would see it looking down from above in a small aircraft.

It was nighttime, the city was completely lit up and he managed in distinguishing the headlights of the moving vehicles that occupied the LA highways and city streets.

John felt very light, very light but nevertheless his feet did not leave the ground. In the midst of the night, while savoring this view from above, he wobbled along the Pacific coast which boarded Los Angeles. Throughout this time he felt an indescribable inner peace, an impression of sensational body dilatation and felt that he could become as big as he wanted without being heavier.

Nobody seemed to notice him. Incredible when one is so huge.

Even though Solenne had frequently invited John to her home, he had never set foot here prior.

Also, one must remember that having arrived in the middle of the night John could not have any idea as to what was waiting for him at sunrise.

Nevertheless, John wakes up at an early hour. It is eight o'clock and he realizes, with great satisfaction, that he is quite a ways from his little country home.

He gets out of bed and upon opening the opaque curtains that covered the large bedroom window; John discovers a most magnificent view.

At first sight, a few palm trees and an abundance of multicolor flora. Neighboring houses are quite scarce. From the top of this hill he notice the city a distance away. It is still covered with dense clouds that are of such a pure white, it is breathtaking..

A little further away, we can barely distinguish the mountain line which appear to act as an armour protecting this vast angelic city.

The sun's rays fiercely pierce this white mass in an attempt to overpower it.

John believes he is still dreaming and rubs his eyes to confirm the reality of this beautiful scene which is given freely to him.

Filled with amazement, he leaves his room and makes his way towards the living room. He finds Solenne there, coffee at hand and also appears caught up in some sort of divine contemplation.

- *Wonderful, just simply wonderful, it's splendid.* States John unable to keep his impressions within.
- *It's true.* Continues Solenne casually. *I love this place. It's the highest point of elevation in Los Angeles. We can see everything from here. We get the impression of being above all the coming and going that is taking place at this hour.*
- *I have never seen such a captivating scenery.*
- *One of these mornings we will get up very early to see the sun rise and you'll see that it is even more impressive then at this moment. When the sunrise begins, you would believe you're in heaven.*
- *I feel that I will not be lonely here Solenne.*
- *Of course.* States Solenne somewhat morose. *But, unfortunately, I believe that my time allotted to appreciate this view is going to be cut soon.*
- *Really?* Questions John.
- *Yes…with the divorce and Frank's setbacks on the stock market, we'll probably*
- *Have to sell this place.*
- *That's too bad…*
- *Meanwhile, I plan on savoring every moment…would you like some coffee?*

John accepts and as Solenne prepares to serve him, he comfortably sits himself on the couch, facing the big window and fills himself with the beauty of this unimaginable view.

- *It's so weird how I feel right now Solenne.*
- *In what way?*
- *I don't know exactly. I feel a total comfort, as though I were present everywhere in this airytale decor. I feel very light, without any problems, absolutely no concerns, I don't know…*

- *It must be some sort of mystic experience attached to the level of energy found here.*

John reflects a moment in attempting to grasp what Solenne has just said.

- *Did you say a "mystic experience"?* Asks John.
- *Yes. In certain favorable occasions, once we have attained a high level of vibration,we succeed in bringing ourselves above the level of terrestrial vibrations at which time we reach superior levels, approaching us more and more to levels of pure vibrations. It's as though, in full state of consciousness, we reach our divine part, the superior levels of evolution…you remember…*
- *Yeah, those three weird one…bouddic, athmic and…*
- *And Causal…yes, that's it.* Confirms Solenne.
- *It's really beneficial.* States John.
- *Yes, we really feel good during those moments. We almost feel divine. We Feel as though nothing can bypass us. We also feel as though we have an answer for everything.*
- *That's it.* Continues John. *I feel as though I'm connected to such a powerful source*
- *OF energy that I could do anything and succeed at everything.*
- *Connected to the real source, some sort of universal energy.* Replies Solenne.
- *I feel as though I am growing and could grow as much as I wanted to.* Confides John.
- *It's definitely a mystic experience. Everything appears beautiful in those moments.*
- *The only other time I felt something of the sort…*continues John…*is when I went to St-Pierre to see my son. That day I admired everything and liked what I saw, basically it was as though I was one with nature.*

Solenne lets him continue and appears to be preparing a plan in her mind.

- *We are going to take advantage of this moment of extra-lucidity John.*
- *What are we going to do?*
- *An experience.* Continues Solenne.
- *An experiance ?* Questions John.
- *Yes, you will see, it's amusing but especially enriching.*
- *What must I do?*
- *Lets get ready and then I'm going to take you for a car ride.* Replies Solenne amused.
- *A car ride…an experience?*
- *Yes, all you have to do is let the energy pass through you and then give me your impressions as we go along.*

John feels amused by this proposition and so in less than two minutes they are ready to undertake this ride.

Once in the vehicle, Solenne turns off the radio and explains to John that he must simply feel the energy and give her his impressions as they drive along. Solenne was to only listen to his comments and not react until later on.

She had already thought of this particular routing she would take which took them through various different sectors of the city. They would travel through such neighborhoods as high class, low income and the working class, etc.

Eventually, without quite knowing how, John began his comments;

- *It's weird…it's as though…you'll probably be deceived but…I think I lost my state of euphoria. All of a sudden I feel normal again, I would even go as far as saying I don't' feel well. It's as though I could become lugubrious, without any ambitions, something like that...I most certainly flunk the test.*

Solenne smiles and explains the following to John:

- *No, everything is going well.* She begins. *What you are feeling is normal. I would even say you passed with flying colors. I just drove by one of the most disadvantaged neighborhoods of LA. Misery, pain, suffering, poverty, its all there. That is what you felt. You fell to their level of vibrations.*
- *But Solenne, we are on a highway...*Comments John.
- *I know, that is what's so powerful. We didn't even enter the neighborhood. We only drove close to it and you still felt it.* Replies Solenne.

John finally realizes that he can be positive, negative, morose, in ecstasy etc...depending the level of vibration surrounding him, therefore, he returns to his receptive state that he was shortly before.

- *Now, I feel good.* Continues John. *I've become, once again, some sort of Mr Joe Blow.*
- *I feel like going shopping, playing golf, taking a walk in the sun... something of the kind, you know.*

Solenne smiles again and gives the following comments:

- *You see how easy it is, once we have reached a certain degree, to feel people andthings. We are in an area where people come to amuse themselves. Actually, not far from here there is a shopping center, the beach is also only five minutes away and the golf course along with other amusement parks are all in the vicinity.*

- *Wow!* Exclaims John.

John feels great about himself. He feels proud to have finally succeeded the experience. He almost reaches a higher level of euphoria but
then suddenly changes and warns Solenne.

- *Stop the car…* shouts John.
- *What?*
- *Stop the car now! No, actually take the next exit, hurry!*
- *What's wrong John?*
- *I don't know…something serious, I can feel it Solenne, and I also
  feel that we Must hurry. Go on, take that exit.* Exclaims John once
  again impatiently.
- *Go ahead John, guide me.*
- *Here, take a left…no go straight ahead.*

Solenne carefully follows every direction John gives her and they
head in the direction of downtown LA towards the unknown.

- *There, to your right…hurry, hurry.* Continues John.
- *But what are you feeling; do you have an image in you head?*
- *It's got me by the guts Solenne. It practically frightens me. There,
  now it's Getting stronger and stronger. I'm scared, I'm really scared
  but of what?…We're almost there Solenne. That alley…there…just
  in front, it's here.*

In front of them stood a crowd that entirely blocked the alleyway
they had just taken.
Advancing slowly, Solenne has a look of intrigue on her face. John and
Solenne both look at each other with amazement of his own intervention.

- *But what's going on over there?* Wonders Solenne out loud.

- *I don't know any more than you do Solenne, I...I was kind of called or led here.*

More people arrive and gather around a scene that appears to be horrible. Solenne and John exit the vehicle in an attempt to find out more of the situation.

- *And in broad daylight!* Exclaims a terrified woman.

Solenne approaches the crowd and attempts to find out more.

- *What exactly happened...* Asks Solenne to nobody in particular.

A man of a certain age turns towards her and in a degusted voice replies:

- *They shot him...for no reason...a few measly dollars.*
- *But who is he...* Requests Solenne.
- *The owner of that small corner store...he was a good man but those bastards will shoot on you like on empty bottles anyways!* Concludes the stranger in disbelief.

John had remained at the back. He then witnesses something which confuses him even more. He sees the crowd but in the center he notices glimmers of red and white lights releasing themselves and then finally sees a cloud raise itself over the crowd. He also notices that surrounding each person is a shadow of different colors; red, black, gray, yellow and green.
Solenne returns towards John and instructs him to return to the vehicle. John appears to be somewhat lost in his daydreaming.

- *Let's get in the car, right now!* Exclaims Solenne with authority.

John reacts at which moment his vision disappears.

Troubled by this, he questions Solenne in regards to what happened at the scene.

- *An armed robbery gone badly…the guy was killed when he attempted to follow*
- *his aggressors.* Explains Solenne.

At this moment John becomes pale, he feels very ill and requests that they leave immediately.

- *We've got to leave this place, I'm going to faint…I think I've gone too far…I feel*
- *I'm losing control…*

Solenne puts her car in reverse and they rapidly leave the area to finally return towards the quiet and peaceful neighborhood where Solenne lives.

A long moment of silence separates them, each tempting to understand this strange event.

Solenne gradually returns to an acceptable speed and enquiries into John's state.

- *And now?* She begins.
- *I'm okay, I'm okay…I'm getting my senses back.* Replies John.
- *What exactly happened out there John?*
- *I felt it, I knew something serious was about to happen but I didn't know what it*
- *Was about. I know that when I felt it, it had not yet taken place but it was imminent.*
- *I know, but once at the scene, you appeared unconscious…*
- *I thought I was going to pass out.* Explains John.

- *Did you hear or see anything whatsoever?*

On this question John turns towards Solenne and confides the following:

- *I saw…I think I saw some sort of glimmers of light around the crowd and others releasing themselves from the center of the crowd.*

Solenne becomes serious and remains quiet.

- *What does it mean Solenne?*
- *Let's go back to my place, we'll discuss it there…Lets take the time to get over this a bit. We must cool down a little, in some way, calm the spirits; we must find our own vibrations and detach ourselves from all of that.* Replies Solenne.

The remainder of the trip home was done in complete silence. John and Solenne took this time to wind down and soon enough they had reached Solenne's calm and comforting residence.

Upon entering the house, Solenne attempted to relax the mood by opening an unrelated conversation.

- *So, what do you say we go out and rent us a good action movie?*

John bursts into laughter and replies:

- *I've had my share of that for today thank-you. Instead, would you happen to have some herbal tea to help my nerves?*

Solenne invites John to take a seat in the living room and shortly after returns with a kettle of hot water and a box of various herbal teas.

Once calmed down, John opens the discussion and requests some explanation from Solenne.

- *Come on Solenne; tell me what that was all about, you must have some idea?*
- *Finally, it's quite simple.*
- *Simple maybe, but not ordinary.* Comments John.
- Solenne takes a deep breath and begins explaining…*when we left this morning you were in an extreme receptive state of mind. Everything reached you. You could feel everything; therefore, I wanted to be certain that its origin was from your gut and not mental.From my gut?* Wonders John?
- *It's an expression.* Continues Solenne. *You felt it in your guts as one would say; therefore it did not result from an intellectual or rational mental analysis.*
- *You can be sure…it was from my gut all right! It almost made me puke…*
- *Good. It's also what we call "feeling with your heart". Feeling things and people.*
Adds Solenne.
- *I wouldn't want to disagree but I had the impression that it did not come from my heart nor my brain…it was more…gastric!*
- *You're right. It comes from some other area but it kind of has to pass through your heart, the heart of our soul.*
- *Oh, okay, the heart of my soul…of course. What was I thinking?* States John jokingly.
- *You see, it does not consist of the heart as we all know it, the one that pumps blood into our veins but…the heart of the soul, basically. It's in relation to the shacras, you know what I mean?*
- *Yes.* Replies John.
- *In these moments, which could be very brief, we have the impression of feeling various particular sensations. We feel we can guess everything but none of it can be verified by the rational. But this event*

that shook us proves very well that it exits. It obviously happened to re-enforce our position on the subject.

- *So, if I understand you correctly, if we could reach this state by simply desiring it, nothing could surprise us and nobody could lie or steal from us; we would guess everything before hand.* Comments John.
- *That's true. The funniest part of it all is that it happens to everyone. Everyone has experienced this during a moment of extra-lucidity but since we are used to living in a world that is too rational and pragmatic, we ignore it and find ourselves later explaining it by stating…"I knew it" I should have guessed it" or even "I should have trusted my gut feeling" etc etc. More often then none, we deny it by saying things such as "no, it's not possible' or "Come on, it's just my imagination playing tricks".* You see, continues Solenne, *we don't really listen to ourselves, and we quickly bring ourselves back to our physical being that is so reassuring. Finally, it's simply a question of transmitting – receiving.*
- *Transmitting…and receiving? Are you talking about sensitive neurons or something of the sort?* Questions John somewhat confused.
- *It has nothing to do with it John. This does not take place on the physical level. The sensitivity neurons of the human body are quite physical but they can only perceive what travels in the physical world, such as heat, cold, hard or soft etc*
- *What about the odors we smell, the noise…they are not physical. We cannot see them.*

Comments John quite intrigued.

- *Well, what about atomic radiation, can you see them?* Replies Solenne in a somewhat arrogant tone. *The physical world has, for quite some time, passed the tactical and visible barriers. Sound travels by waves which our ears are able to detect thanks to phenomenal equipment. But even then, it grasps only a limited amount of frequencies. Our ears cannot capture sounds, which are too low or too high pitched. This is also similar to the fact that our eyes cannot see the different components of white lights, and even less the ultra-violets or infrared lights. Nevertheless, they do also exist. If there existed absolutely no physical components for sound or sights, how could we call each other long distance or watch a television show with equipment that is nothing less then physical.* States Solenne with conviction.

- *You're so right Solenne, I don't know much on that subject I guess.*

John stops himself short and pretends he understands but his curiosity pushes him to try and find out more.

- *Okay then, what we do receive comes from where?* Continues John.
- *From the universal energetic field.*
- *What is that?* Questions John quite interested.
- *Well, as you know, we are composed of the physical body but also of some more subtle layers that are formed from energy but they are subtle energetic bodies compared to your body which is a dense energetic mass. That is why all our bodily "tools" can intervene but when it comes to the subtle layers, none of our "tools" can perceive them or even less succeed in influencing them, at least not for the moment anyways. These subtle bodies have great properties and much greater and stronger capacities then that of our physical body.*
- *What you are saying is that we have invisible ears, mouth and heart?* Asks John in an innocent way.
- *If you want to put it that way, sure. But, where it becomes interesting is that all actions or reactions of the subtle bodies will echo on our physical body and then, and only then, will we feel physical vibrations.*
- *Like fear, joy or pain?* Continues John. *The blood pressure which may rise or lower, the cardiac rhythm that diminishes or increases...*
- *Exactly. The physical body reacts and it could either be beneficial or unhealthy.*
Explains Solenne.

Still attempting to fully comprehend, John tries a new comparison.

- *Like the peel on an orange; if we remove it, the orange will rot and if we nourish it the orange will develop itself.*
- *It's something of the sort John.*
- *Therefore, we also unknowingly receive a lot of interference, right?*
- *For the moment, yes, because we are not yet aware of this but when the day comes when science acknowledges this state of being, we will begin working on it and life will get easier for everyone. That is when the traditional interventions that we do on our physical body will lose their place. We will have to redo everything; from the medical field to our means of transportation.*
- *So, if I felt very light then tired and then with the desire to amuse myself, was it because I was feeling the effects of these energetic fields, as you say? Asks John.*
- *Exactly…exclaims Solenne. You were a…receiver. You caught everything in your way. You vibrated in the same rhythm as the fields which surrounded you. You let yourself be navigated in these fields following their course. You abandoned yourself to the surrounding energetic forces and when you became too week, it was because you reached a level which was too low for you to rise on your own from. Actually, just like a radio; the radio is happy or sad if the waves it receives are happy or sad.*
- *So we had to go in an area that is energetically greater!* Exclaims John quite pleased.
- *Actually, once there, you gradually recuperated and regained control of your own energy. Also like a light bulb would; if you diminish the electricity feeding it, it will dim and become pale, just as you did earlier. Adds Solenne Jokingly.*
- *But Solenne, that is saying that we are not masters of our taste or envies.*
- *We attempt to be but don't accomplish it very well since we are not working on the proper plan.*

- *But I can very well, for example, listen to someone's list of miseries and then return home whistling, without feeling concerned* . Comments John.
- *It's a good thing; otherwise you would also end up with a pharmacy filled with medication.*
- *But does that mean that when I don't' feel concerned…*
- *That you block your personal energetic field, that you remain in complete control of yourself?* Interrupts Solenne completing his thought. *Yes, you can listen to someone, that is when you are a receiver, but you don't store his or her negative energy. You immediately return them to the surrounding environment. You can feel what the person is telling you without being trapped in their energetic field. Do you understand John?*
- *Yes…It's very simple as you put it.* Replies John while rubbing his head.
- *We are all searching for energy. We are all linked by energetic fields. One day I will refer a few books for your reading John. But, since we have not learned to draw from this inexhaustible universal source, we attempt to take it from others around us. This is what pushes us to go and tell them about our problems, to discredit what another person may have said or done. The person who reacts to our attacks, as discrete as they may be, loses energy and we grasp hold of it.* Explains Solenne quite seriously.
- *I guess it's almost the same thing as when we take control of a discussion; once it's done we feel somewhat powerful and after tell ourselves "Boy, did I get him".*
- *Yes and then the other person crawls home, week, and will himself regain energy by going to another person and doing the same thing. An example would be the parent who yells at his children when they return home from work or even just by listening to music and trying to relax, this is to regain some energy. There are also those who attempt to escape their sad reality by consuming too much alcohol,*

punching out walls or even by getting stoned. They channel their negative energy on objects, alcohol or drugs. Continues Solenne.

- *So that's what universal energy really is, a never-ending battle.* Comments John quite proud of having understood.
- *True, and it will remain as such for as long as we haven't comprehended that instead of emptying people around us we should simply connect ourselves to the appropriate areas to refill our energy.*
- *This would be like whenever I meet someone and upon leaving that discussion I say, "every time I meet that person he just drains me completely" and feel exhausted so I never want to talk with him for more than ten minutes. This means they used me and took my energy.* Continues John in a very satisfied mood.
- *Exactly.* Confirms Solenne.
- *Would it be the same thing but in reverse when we feel energized by someone?* Then questions John.
- *Just as true but it could also mean that it is this other person who is being drained.*
- *Watch yourself and notice the other person's attitude. You could yourself become an energy "taker". We get easily caught up by it, it's so accessible and requires very little effort.*
- *But what if the other person is just as energized, as in "love at first sight"?* Further questions John.
- *At that moment, it is that both are in an extreme ecstatic moment and that both your levels of energy meet and become one, as when you put two flames together. This causes a spark and then an electrifying short-circuits which is felt by both parties.*
- *If we could actually see what takes place at such a moment we would really see energetic fields entangling themselves together to become a small electrical storm*

Solenne interrupts herself and awaits a reaction from John.

- *You said, if we could see it? Begins John.*
- *Yes.*
- *Because…it's probably…*
- *What you saw this morning John at the shooting. You did see energetic fields.*

Continues Solenne.

Confused, John continues looking for explanations.

- *But you yourself earlier said that our eyes could not…*
- *The question is "where you in our world at that moment John?"*
- *No, it's true. I was somewhere else, as we often say. I was…daydreaming, elsewhere, not really there. Realizes John.*
- *And you were in a receptive state to be envied by all. But also, when I interrupted you the image disappeared, did it not?*
- *Yeah, its true Solenne, by then I could only see what we see ordinarily.*
- *You simply became conscious; you lost your state of supra-consciousness John. You became yourself but…emptied.*
- *Maybe it was just a hallucination after all Solenne.*
- *Ah, that word again! Used when we are unable to explain events by our actual knowledge…as of this moment, discard this word from your vocabulary.*
- *So what you are actually saying Solenne, is that the colored clouds that I saw were real*
- *On a different level than we presently know, absolutely. Certain people call it an aura. Thanks to the perception of an aura we can know if a person is well intentioned, irritated, happy or even sick.*
- *Wait a minute. Interrupts John excitedly. You've just reminded me of an event.*
- *What is it?*
- *You remember my dream…sorry, I mean my out of body experience I had on the plane?*
- *Of course John, you told me all about it already, why?*

- *During this experience I saw a small gray cloud over a woman's breast...would it mean...*
- *Obviously some sort of physical medical problem. Grey represents an energy loss, a blockage of some sort. That's how it's described anyways!* Explains Solenne.
- *An infection...*
- *Possible. It could even be a tumor maybe...it could have been interesting to question her, but finally...*
- *It's incredible...I'm learning so much Solenne.*

John becomes pensive and then attempts to take the discussion even deeper.

- *Therefore,* he begins, *we are fighting for energy that we are steeling amongst each other but there exists an inexhaustible source that is inaccessible by our present methods.*
- *Bull's eye John.*
- *But what is true for two individuals, is it also true for two populations Solenne?*
- *Unfortunately yes.*
- *And so they're also...the wars, the revolutions....*
- *Yes John. Pain having become necessary when two populations or groups have mutually exhausted themselves by robbing the available energy of the other. This said, they have exhausted their energy and have descended, in some sort, the vibrations, which united them to the point of creating what comes from such low vibrations like disharmony, quarrels, conflicts, and war. All that for nothing. Sometimes I find myself laughing alone when I'm listening to the news and they state that such a county is in conflict with another country...It makes me think of the following image; put two dogs in a barrel, then you put a very small piece of meat in it too. The barrel has to be high enough for the dogs to be able to get out of it with ease*

but so that they cannot see what is outside surrounding it. Then, all around the barrel you put enough meat to feed one hundred dogs for five years. Afterwards, you just watch what happens. What do you think is going to happen John?

- *Simple. They are both going to waste a lot of energy arguing. Only one will be permitted to eat that single piece and it will only suffice to give him back the energy he has just lost while the other has to content himself in observing the first one enjoy his meat.*
- *Basically, if we add and subtract the energy lost and found, we find ourselves in the red. This is how we regress instead of advancing in life. We just keep finding ourselves without sufficient energy.*
- *I guess that is how us humans are. Like dumb dogs who believe they are stuck in a cage and by wanting to take everything the other has, we forget what lies ahead. If we did just a small effort to see what is on the outside of the barrel.... enough meat for everyone! Real animals!*

John appears having completely understood it all but concludes with these last remarks.

- *Why the different aura colors?*
- *Like the rainbow John.*
- *Ah...I'm supposed to understand that, is that it?*
- *The rainbow John...red, orange, yellow, green, blue, purple, violet and indigo...*
- *What about the rainbow, Solenne?*
- *The higher you go, the better it is, the prettier it is, less irritating if you want.*
- *Wait a minute, if I see a red aura around a person, does that mean that his vibrations are...low?*
- *Somewhat so John. Red is a lower frequency than the blue for example,.. I guess your parallel has some sense to it. Red would be associated with anger, irritation...do you see? Very low feelings.*

- *So Solenne, a person in perfect harmony would release what color, violet?*
- *No, it would more likely be white...*
- *I see. But there isn't any white in the rainbow Solenne...*
- *There, you are being to intellectual John, we could do parallels but it would be wrong for us to bring all back to the physical plan. Anyways, isn't white the union of all the colors brought together? The union of all the colors of the rainbow.*
- *Yeah...a person with a white light could then have access to all the frequencies, in some sort.*
- *That must be it John...we still don't know much on this subject.*
- *What about the black Solenne?*

Solenne smiles and continues.

- *Black...it's the absence of color John. Think of absolutely no lights. NO FREQUENCIE.* Replies Solenne satisfied with herself and bursts out laughing.

John feels he has reached the limits of Solenne's knowledge but his stubborn curiosity refuses to quit.

- *I'm sure that there is someone who could answer us...we must not be the only people studying this phenomenon...*
- *I know some people who may be able to help us John. If you want to, maybe we will go see them some day soon.*

Eleventh Chapter

The days that followed were much more quiet. Solenne and john decided to simply take advantage of their time together.

They rested at the beach, visited the neighboring cities, and took walks on the boardwalk: basically simply enjoying each other's company and relaxing.

During this time, they exchanged thoughts and amused themselves by passing non-disrespectful comments on the people they saw. They never attempted to find these people's true reason for being or their level of interpersonal relations.

As they were sipping a coffee on a lovely terrace of Sunset Boulevard, Solenne suggested they amuse themselves and take advantage of some of the local attractions.

- *You must surely want to see some of our tourist attractions.* States Solenne.
- *And what would you recommend?* Continues John without any real interest.
- *I don't know, there is Sea World, the Movie Industries...there are plenty of things to see, you just have to chose...*

John does not appear to react and remains indifferent.

- *As you can see, I'm too old for those things Solenne. It's probably very interesting but it no longer interests me.* Replies John.
- *Maybe some other time then.*

Solenne and John remain there a few more minutes appreciating the beautiful day and simply observing the people around them going about their daily routines and occupations.

- *I really don't feel as though I belong in this world,* comments John, *I get tired just watching them run about.*
- *Yeah…*acknowledges Solenne.
- *I also feel like this in regards to the attraction sites you mentioned. How would I put it…it's…it's without…it doesn't have any interest for me, I don't quite know how to say it but it is as though I cannot see what they could do for me.*
- *It's simply because you no longer need them John. But, they are still very useful for the general population. Many people find some comfort in these places.*
- *The exchange of energy in public places is sensational. Of course though, to fill all these people we must put the maximum.*
- *What do you mean by that?* Questions John.
- *Well, let's take money, okay? Money is a type of energy in itself.*
- *I suppose so.* Continues John.
- *Have you ever seen money in your dreams John?*
- *Of course!*
- *You see, the language of dreams is still close to reality. In a dream, money represents energy.*
- *I see where you're coming from Solenne.*
- *People need energy…we talked about this the other day. To be able to give them some we must have plenty of it and that requires a large*

group of people; those in charge and the employees of these attraction sites for example, as well as all the shows put on to satisfy them.

- *So, what you are trying to say Solenne is that a movie, a theatre show or people throwing a ball around a field are themselves a source of energy.*
- *Of course. We go there to observe them, we replenish ourselves and these people are there, in front of us, spreading an incredible quantity of their efforts, therefore their energy. After such shows, haven't you noticed how we feel energized?* Questions Solenne.
- *It's so true. But, how do they replenish themselves though? If I were to continue on you stream of thought, if a person can empty the energy of another, a crowd could easily exterminate an entire football team in just one game.* Replies John laughing.
- *But people pay for that John. Paying to receive someone's energy is somewhat a sort of mutual contract respecting the natural universal laws thus applied to the physical plan. When you encounter someone who, without warning, robs you of your energy, it is that she/he took it without your consent and especially because you were not expecting it.*
- *I'm doing some thinking as you talk and I believe you are right Solenne. I'm imagining myself listening to one of my sisters-in-law, a real energy sucker that one is, and if she were to give me a twenty-dollar bill, it could maybe lighten the fatigue I have in listening to her.*
- *Psychiatrists know this very well. How do you think they manage to listen to everyone's miseries and not find themselves on the verge of suicide every night? They are paid for it, as are doctors, lawyers, plumbers, cleaning ladies, the newspaper delivery person…actually, everyone. People are willing to send their energy to others but request some in return. The fact to, in return, give them a piece of*

paper, money, it brings a standard to the energetic transactions. States Solenne.

- *Therefore, the fact of being paid for an important amount of energy given in a short period of time is sufficient to refill us?* Continues John.
- *Sometimes yes, but on other occasions we use this sort of energy, which is money, to complete our own resources. For example, when after a hard day's work you attend a restaurant and purchase yourself a good meal. Even though we had been given money, it was not sufficient to give us our resources. Therefore, the money was reused to find this energy somewhere else. So, money is only a vehicle for energy.*
- *So Solenne, if we do something without being paid, we are short somewhere.*
- *Not if you were prepared for it John.*
- *You keep talking about being prepared for it. What do mean exactly?* Questions John.
- *Let me give you an example. Let's say that you do volunteer work for underprivileged children. You will live many different emotions, feelings, you will have to do physical efforts etc. It is certain that you will spend a lot of energy.*
- *I'm listening.* Continues John intrigued.
- *Yet, when you leave there you will feel less emptied than if your boss had asked you to do an hour of overtime without being paid. Don't you agree John?*
- *Weird…but true.* Replies John.
- *You might even feel more energized then when you arrived there. You now understand why John.*
- *Because I decided to give my energy, I agreed to it and was not surprised by it.*
- *That's it; you were actually prepared for it. Also, when we prepare ourselves to give energy without receiving money in return, we actually fill ourselves with the required energy before leaving. This way, we will*

not leave there exhausted. You know what John, there also exists another way to prepare ourselves without ever being emptied…

- *I can't see how.* Replies John in a pensive manner.
- *Simple,* continues Solenne, *you connect yourself to the universal source of energy, it is bottomless, but that one, people do not yet use it on a conscious level. Some actually do use it but are not aware that they do. They accomplish an extreme amount of tasks without exhausting themselves and then declare that they do not feel tired. It is because they had, unconsciously, connected themselves to this inexhaustible source.*
- *But Solenne, money is not the only way of recuperating other people's energy.*
- *Fortunately, otherwise we would always be in shortage, as you put it. This is also why I explained that you could also feel stronger when you accomplished a task which was non lucrative. The satisfaction of having helped someone is one, happiness, joy, gratitude received by others; they are all very important sources of energy.*
- *Evidently, nature is also filled with energy. Listening to the sound of a stream, to be marveled by a garden, to lean on a tree and feel its strength etc., to admire a sunset, these are all inexhaustible sources of energy. But, this return of energy is done in the unseen and frequently people don't realize what they have just accomplished. They feel it and keep going back to that source when needed but do not realize the entire energetic mechanism which they employed. The day where we begin doing it consciously, we will practically become invisible, inexhaustible, and invulnerable. We must also be as welcoming to this form of energy as we would be to the amount written on a check. The energy transported by emotions is worth much more then money. Actually, I was going to ask you something. You talk about emotions, sentiments; for you, this is money?* Wonders John.
- *But of course John. But be careful, we can rob you of your money but we can also rob you of your emotions.*

- *Explain that one to me Solenne.*
- *For example, you help me paint a wall. Once the work complete I pay you a meal and a bear. You feel rewarded. As soon as you have your back turned I spread the word that you are unbelievably slow as a painter, that you are so messy and that the work would have been done better without you. You get wind of this and feel irritated, literally pisssed off and feel your pride has been hurt. You feel quite insulted, belittled and cheated, somewhat destroyed. Your meal and beer are no longer worth much next to this, don't they John?*
- *It's true, I would feel extremely emptied. Unless…unless I don't waste any time with these comments of yours.*
- *Therefore John, as I was saying, feelings and emotions are a form of transportation for energy that is more powerful than money. This is why we have to learn to live above our emotions and feelings.*
- *You are talking about negative energy such as anger, hate, envy; but what about the others such as joy, happiness, and serenity?* Questioned John.
- *They are also carriers of energy but they obviously fill us and not empty us. Therefore we should search for these John.*
- *I surprised you there, didn't I Solenne? Tourist attractions are therefore a good choice to get some resources.*
- *I suppose if one has not yet learned to connect to the real source, to concentrate on you, it would be a good choice John. But, I believe that you have passed this step otherwise you would have accepted my offer earlier. It is that these various outlets would not be able to bring you on a higher level then you already are.*
- *At this particular level, one does not react to negative nor positive emotions, to negative or positive feelings; we become centered on ourselves, on our own energy.*
- *But life must be so dark without any ups or downs.* Comments John.
- *You mean without any downs. We always remain in the highs. There comes a time where we cannot go any higher on the physical plan. If*

you augment the vibrations of your subtle layers, you body will feel the positive effects and will react John. Fewer sicknesses, less emotional troubles and less problems. Then comes the time where you reach a certain summit which, if you succeeded in passing it, on the etherique plan of course, your physical body would be nothing but overcharged, under this ultimate energetic tension and would become in an effervescent state, it would sort of wipe itself out. It would begin vibrating at the rhythm of superior levels and…theoretically…you would disappear John.

John burst out in laughter and then difficultly regains his calm trying to encourage Solenne to continue.

- *Forgive me Solenne; my imagination got the better of me…*
- *Well, once you have reached this point, absolutely no emotion, not even the most wonderful news one could receive, could bring you on a higher level. You have already reached it.*
- *Wait a minute; I just got a vision in my head…It would be as though we became little suns. The sun is a ball of immeasurable energy. I'm applying what you have just said and I'm trying to imagine what negative energy could reach it to weaken it and which positive energy could reach to make it brighter, impossible! I don't know of any form of energy strong enough to do this, even the atomic bomb is nothing but a small firecracker next to the sun.*
- *The image is a good one John. You have this gift of bringing everything said into examples, in images actually.*
- *That's because I'm a dreamer Solenne, and don't forget it.* States John amusingly.
- *So, therefore John, you see that money is only that. Energy. What you have you gained by using you own energy. This is all that society has found, for the moment, to help permit us to manage our energy. We*

exchange it, we get some back, we accumulate it, we spend it, we invest it; but we cannot live without it. One day money will also be useless.

- *Therefore Solenne, can one say that the richer we are financially, the more evolved we are...something like that?*
- *Not at all John. One could be what I call "human garbage" and be rich but this money, which is somewhat stolen or acquired in dishonesty, then becomes a loan and not a gain. The interests accumulate very quickly and the day will come where, it could take an entire lifetime or even two...you will have to re-reimburse this amount. At that moment, you'd better be ready because the tab will be extremely high.*
- *But Solenne, when I worked for the government, I saw many people richen themselves fraudulently and they appeared to be living a good life.*
- *Wasn't there any sickness, or misfortune such as a home burning down, a forbidding son, no enemies that didn't stop harassing them...come-on, it's impossible John. Just simply impossible. They are also subject to the universal laws. And also, in this world we pay our debts in various manners.*
- *I guess it's true. They always appeared caught up in some unbelievable stories but...when I saw them in their huge boats or comfortably seated in their limousines, I kept telling myself...*
- *That is all nothing but air John, dust in our eyes. What they show the world is only in an attempt to be envied by others but the invisible world has an eye on them and cannot be fooled by their games.*
- *Therefore, too much money is not compatible with the progression of evolution? Asks John.*
- *Not at all, but I can tell you this, if one day you become extremely rich, it better be due to your good and honest work.*
- *But Solenne, since you appear to say that the bible is a source of directives to be followed, as long as we properly understand it, it clearly states; "You have but one master; God or money".*
- *Come on John, you can yourself very clearly interpret this passage.*

- *Sorry, I thought you were being the devil's advocate. But finally, people don't really run after money, they are running after energy… without knowing it.*
- *That's it, the money, which they are seeking, forbids them from seeing their genuine energetic source, the invisible part, their divine part. Finally, you yourself have answered your question John.*
- *Therefore…if you let money control you, if you make it your master, you forget your divine part and then are no longer your own master.*
- *That's it.* States Solenne somewhat disengaged from this discussion.

John contemplates a while over this short exchange they had and concludes.

- *It becomes evident. It is not wrong to have money but it is to make it an object of adoration that is wrong..*
- *Exactly. If you become more pure and that your actions as your words are well oriented towards helping humanity, you will always have enough of it. Money will come to you, as you need air to breath John.*
- *To help humanity.* States John while letting out a sigh.
- *Help your neighbor and you will be helping humanity. It is not necessary to save an entire nation. If we each help one person, humanity will be saved. Did He not say, " What you do to the smallest of mine, you do onto me" and "love thy neighbor as yourself"?*
- *Yes he did Solenne…which means…*
- *You yourself, are a divine part, agree.*
- *That's it, I'm God…*states John wanting to add a little humor in their discussion.
- *Exactly. Therefore, if you hurt someone, you lower his energy, you remove money and you build a dept for yourself, an energetic dept; you've just begun a loan of your own. The balance is quite negative since we are all part of this superior divine plan that we must find.*

Finally, each bad gesture, each bad word brings us further from the divine plan and brings you further also. The opposite is also true. Act and talk positively and we keep getting closer to the divine plan.

- *Basically, when He stated this phrase, he was talking about your divine plan, as though your subtle layers were talking to you. Written differently we could say; "what you do wrong to others is an interference for you, what good you do to others, you will receive its profits."*

In a mocking tone of voice, John states the following.

- *So all I have to do is wait and in not too long I should receive a big check because I believe I'm living a good and honest life.*
- *If only it were so simple John.* Continues Solenne. *Money can fall upon you at any moment like it could never happen either. When you do something good or say something good, you could also be banking it or maybe just paying a previous debt, sometimes even very old debts…but continue to do good, to work on yourself and to look for the truth and if nothing else, your balance sheet we keep getting more positive.*
- *I was only joking Solenne. But, would this explain why certain people appear to have all the luck in the world at their side and others lose everything they worked for?*
- *We would have to take this reflection to a much deeper level but I would say yes, it could be explained in this manner, at least with these notions. Every case is to be taken separately John.*
- *That would be like that man we saw on television the other day who had bought a lottery ticket, the fist one of his life. He lost it with his wallet and the guy who found it brought it back to him without knowing the ticket had the winning numbers.*
- *In the same case, the man asks the delivery boy to bring his ticket to the store and check the numbers for him. The young boy returns with his items and his ticket accompanied with the list of winning num-*

bers. The young boy did not have the reflex of checking out the man's numbers himself. The man looks at the list and in less than two seconds, becomes a millionaire. I just couldn't believe it.

- *There are certain situations like that John. We cannot judge them. We don't know them. Had he been a missionary during a previous life…who knows. We have given him his due with interests, that's all. To win or inherit a certain amount of money can also be a test we have to go through.*
- *I sure would like that kind of test.* States John in an ironic tone.
- *Understand one thing John. If for you money only has a physical aspect and if you believe that if you were to have a lot of it all your problems would be solved, this favor of providence will sooner or later, disillusion you; some sort of message from destiny that wants to have you understand that material possession is not the goal of life, that beyond money there is something else. The world is filled with rich people who are miserable.*
- *But in conclusion Solenne, isn't it selfish to keep it all to yourself?*
- *Not at all John. Anyways, when one has reached a certain degree of evolution sufficiently elevated, this mountain of money is of no value to you. You only see it as a payback for your efforts. You will not rejoice from it as simple luck. You will, nonetheless, know that this energy is to be used to help you continue your work that is to help others advance in their path.*
- *By doing what?* Asks John.
- *It could be just anything. Opening a school, improve on their conditions of life…opening a therapy center; it could also be by doing absolutely nothing.*
- *Nothing…*
- *Yes John…nothing. Acting as an example. People will admire your success and attempt to find the key to such success. When you will answer them that all you did was to obey the universal laws, some*

will want to fallow you example. This is even greater than any school or therapy center.

John and Solenne were still seated at their table and as they were taking a moment of silence, a man, seated nearby, who was indiscreetly listening to their conversation, passed the following comment.

- *Excuse me miss. I happened to overhear.*
- *Go right ahead.* Replies Solenne.
- *According to what you have been saying, the day where everyone will be connected to this natural source, as you put it, we will no longer need money, there will not be enough to reward everyone anyways, we will no longer need the theatres to "recharge" ourselves, the cinemas, not even lawyers, handymen, food, or doctors, finally…this seems extremely absurd to me.*

Solenne realizes that this man still has a long ways to go and does not want to crush his curiosity that could actually be the beginning of his personal search but does not what him to believe that their sayings could only be a fable.

She reflects a moment and asks for inspiration. Then she continues.

- *It's true; it's unthinkable, not in this world in which we presently live in anyways.*

She then takes an amused look and concludes.

- *I must have been talking about another world.*

Disturbed by this intrusion, John and Solenne pay their bill and leave the bistro while saluting the man.

Solenne withholds her laughter and John quickly whispers to her.

- *Why didn't you put him in his place? You would have shredded him in less than two seconds Solenne.*
- *Never mind John. You have to accept that there are others who are on their way. We must certainly not destroy their present principles which are their starting point. You cannot impose it. And, furthermore, do you honestly believe that I needed to waste energy on a lost cause...*

They both burst out laughing and take the route heading for home.

Twelfth chapter

Once the night arrived, Solenne and John agree to go to bed early. John is still under the effect of the different time zones and Solenne would really like John to be able to admire the sunrise from this magnificent viewpoint which is her home.

- *Let's go to bed John, we will get up very early tomorrow. We will take advantage of a morning that is supposed to be clear to observe the sunrise. You'll see, it is such a beautiful show.*
- *I accept. This will permit me to put my clock up to date because I still feel as though I'm two hours late...*

Solenne turns off the living room lights and as John was about to disappear in his bedroom, she adds.

- *I almost forgot John. Tomorrow we will also meet a friend of mine. I'm not telling you more. He will teach us more notions because I believe I'm at the end of my knowledge.*
- *Great, I accept.*

As every other night that preceded an important event, John has an unusual dream which is to be unforgettable.

He finds himself in a very dense tropical forest.

He is alone and in a territory completely unknown to him. He is there, standing and listening to the intimidating sounds of a wild forest. He can feel that life surrounds him but cannot see anything. He turns in every direction as to protect himself from an unknown danger.

Then, he feels even more threatened. He looks for a shelter and as he tumbles into a deep ravine, he observes a space ship flying above him. He feels hunted, so he sticks to the ground even more in an attempt to camouflage himself. Then, another space ship arrives, and another. There are approximately thirty of them there.

This terrifies John. He feels that if he shows himself he will be attacked, taken out of where he can cause trouble. Yet, he cannot figure out why the occupants of these space ships are looking for him.

After a long moment of fear and horror, the ships leave the area without ever having noticed him and then John cautiously exits his hiding place.

He then instantly finds himself in an area where he is well seen and where the trees are far apart from each other. The ground is covered in a rich green carpet and the birds are accompanying him in his travel. He follows a stream which, paradoxically, heads up the hill.

He arrives at the end of the stream and finds himself in a magnificent clearing where several men and woman which are dressed white and who are savoring various fruits, juices and vegetables, are gathered together. A soft music is playing but coming from nowhere in particular. John could also smell sweet odors of perfume quite unfamiliar to him.

At the same moment, he notices Solenne who arrives facing him, across the garden, but by a different trail.

As he was about to hail Solenne, a man of a certain age signals them to come forward and states.

- *Come join us, I will introduce you to your friends. The festivities will soon begin, a little while longer and you would have been late...but we were waiting for you.*

At five o'clock in the morning, John's alarm clock sounds off and wakes him.

He opens his eyes but remains in his bed for a moment. He still has this dream fresh in his mind. He hesitates but then once again takes his manuscript and makes his annotations.

In the living room, which is located back to John's bedroom, Solenne is already seated with a warm cup of herbal tea.

She believes having heard John's movements and, in a friendly manner, states.

- *Time to get up Mr sunshine, you are late.*

Still in bed, John smiles, clearly seeing the allusion Solenne is making to their discussion of the night before, so he gets up and joins her.

- *It's still quite early Solenne.*
- *Yeah, but it's really worth it, you'll see.*

These exchanges are done in a very discrete tone, low voiced, as though both feared disturbing this perfect order that was installing itself slowly.

John took a moment to describe his dream to Solenne.

She appears to rejoice of this dream but John does not even attempt for one moment to find its true sense. He is too caught up in the show that will soon start.

Suddenly John gets up and comments.

- *So this is what I would have missed…it's fantastic Solenne.*

Solenne remains seated and admires this scene from her position.

- *Can't you see it, can't you feel all the energy that is spreading slowly on the city John?*
- *Certainly, and believe it or not, this show repeats itself each morning, unbelievable.*

From the living room we can see the black of night slowly make way for the first orange rays of the morning sun.

In the background, the mountains stand straight as to prevent the thick fog from invading the city and destroying the scenery.

Daylight slowly engulfs the city and beneath this rainfall of energy, the streetlights become more discrete one by one.

The trees and the birds appear to take their ease and attempt to feed themselves of this energetic flux erupting on the city which gives it such life.

Also, the Pacific Ocean bathes the coast as to complete the morning wash that nature gives itself regularly.

This enchainment takes place in a magically slow pace but we can feel that the forces involved only have as adversary, time, who is also giving way.

Once the show concluded, John addresses Solenne to know what the day's schedule entitled.

- *I'm taking you to see a wonderful friend. You'll see, he's really special John.*
- *What does he do exactly?*

- *Oh, not much. He lives secluded in a small Mexican village and keeps busy mostly with his writing.*
- *He's a writer?* Questions John.
- *In some way, yes. He has his degree in philosophy and theology. He spent many years teaching in a local school. There, he occupied an important position in the school's direction and then some day they just never heard from him again.*
- *But then, how do you know that he lives in that village Solenne?*
- *Oh, chanced circumstances. Last year I went to Mexico to rest and I met him in a 'tiengue''.*
- *A what?*
- *A tiengue John. That is how we say flea market in Spanish, at least that's how I believe it's called.*
- *But, it's far form here.*
- *We will fly there. It's a small village, on the pacific coast, quite near Manzanillo. It's a village where the people live from the agriculture, hand made crafts and fishing.*
- *But what is he doing in such a lost place?*
- *That area inspires him, at least so he's told me.*
- *When are we supposed to catch our flight? Asks John with great curiosity.*
- *Later this morning. We will be using a friends plane that I barrowed. Her pilot, Luis, is actually waiting for my call.*
- *It excites me.* I believe I'm really going to like this Solenne.

By the stroke of twelve, noon, Solenne and John find themselves onboard a small plane flying over the coast, in the direction of Manzanillo.

The flight lasts about two hours and, finally, Luis lands at the Manzanillo airport.

While saluting their pilot, Solenne and John pass the customs gate.

They have barely made it across when a customs agent stops them. He addresses them in Spanish and with little Spanish that Solenne knows, she succeeds in understanding him.

- *Your papers please!*

The man appears austere and not too sympathetic.
John expresses his impressions to Solenne.

- *I don't feel comfortable with this. What do they want with us Solenne?*
- *Quiet, I'll explain later John.*

The agent examines their passports and invites them to follow him into a small room without windows.

- *You've just arrived from the United States?* Asks the man rudely.
- *Yes, and we should be here only for one day.* Answers Solenne.
- *But what are you doing here and why only one day?*

John is becoming worried and asks Solenne for answers.

- *What is it that they want Solenne?*
- *They want to know why we are here.*

Becoming quite inpatient John attempts to answer them in English but Solenne immediately interrupts him.

- *What did your friend want to say there?* Asks the agent in a strict tone of voice.
- *He does not speak Spanish and is simply worried of this formality which is unusual for him but be certain that I understand well…so many things happen these days.* Innocently replies Solenne.

- *Are you here to see someone?* Continues the agent.
- *No, just a trip of leisure. I love this place and since my brother was visiting I suggested we come spend a day or two here.*
- *Earlier you said it was just for one day...*interrupts the agent.
- *That will depend on the fun we'll be having.* Replies Solenne a little ironically.

The custom agent verifies their papers once again and inscribes a note on their passports.

Solenne and John regain their papers and leave the small room followed by the unsatisfied look of the agents who did not appear content with Solenne's answers.

Overtaken by these events, John request to know more.

- *The local people are worried John. There are more and more Americans, Canadians and Europeans who arrive here and leave after two or three days. The Mexican authorities, political and religious, are on their guard. They believe it may be an infiltration or revolution being set up, but that has nothing to do with it.*
- *But why are all those people coming here then?*
- *Pointless to talk about it now John, you will understand in a few hours. Let's wait to be on neutral territory!*

John remains unsatisfied and feels somewhat threatens without knowing why. He comforts himself with Solenne's presence and hopes to get to the bottom of this very quickly.

Once outside the airport, they hail a taxi cab to go to the small locality of Barra de Navidad, found at about forty minutes drive from there.

Using the little Spanish that she knows, Solenne addresses the driver.

- *Nosotros queremos ir in la Barra de Navidad por favor.*
- *Si, si senora.*

- *Cuantos minutos por ir ?*
- *Cerca de quarenta y cinco senora.*
- *Gracias. Vamos. Mi nombre es Solenne.*
- *Yo soy Alphonso, senora.*

John had never been to Mexico. Recovered from his disturbed emotion of the airport, he had become like a child while observing each individual as they drove by, also every small house and already felt as though he was in a world different from what he has known so far.

- *I feel that the people here are very honest Solenne.* Comments John. *I feel a very relaxed energy, very fluid. I feel that the people here are very welcoming. I haven't spoken to anyone but already feel reassured.*
- *What you are saying is true John. It is a part of Mexico where the people are very pious and respectful.*
- *I feel as though I am greeted with dignity and consideration. I can now say that I understand your friend. It has to be quite easy to do some writing here when the energy is so available. Oh, by the way, what is his name?* Asks John.
- *Leopold, Leopold Maddock. You may have read one or two of his articles which are laying about on my coffee table.*
- *That was him!* Exclaims John. *He appears to be a very wise man.*
- *Hum…hum…*continues Solenne somewhat pensive.
- *The article on toxic people…it was him?*
- *Yes.*
- *I adored this article Solenne. It is so true; there are more toxic persons than we care to admit.*
- *Yes, but, they do not see themselves that way.*
- *I know Solenne. I found it quite amusing when I saw the drawing, at the beginning of his text, where there is a devil looking in a mirror and his reflection is an angel…this image says it all.*
- *Did you also read the text on individualism and personalities?*

- *That was fantastic Solenne. I would have had trouble making the difference if I had not read this article. It is so true that our personality does not at all reflect our individuality.*
- *And yet…*
- *Yes,…people so easy confuse the two.* Continues John.
- *With his education and the numerous readings he has done, Leopold has reached the maximum in personal evolution John. He is, what I call, an initiated, some kind of shaman as in the antique populations.*
- *An "initiated" and a "shaman"?* Questions John.
- *Yes, a person who has reached wisdom, who constantly lives in the universal love with a pure soul. The shamans represent re-incarnated Gods. It was said that they could communicate with the Gods.*
- *The initiated are the direct link between the invisible world and our world.*
- *Well, why does he live in hiding then Solenne?*
- *He doesn't live in hiding John, he searches for the areas where he can best perform his influences. But, for the moment his work must remained unsuspected. We must attempt to not be followed otherwise it could bring him great problems with the authorities that do not understand any of this.*
- *But what does he act on then, if not politics and religions?*

Solenne remains silent for a moment and then continues.

- *He acts on the people, on the universal energy, that will undoubtedly one day affect the order already established and threaten the present structures…but finally, we are not here to do politics. We simply came here to meet with him, simply for the two of us.*

Arrived at Barra de Navidad, Solenne pays the cab fare and leaves a generous tip. The driver thanks her in a very friendly manner which is typical of the local people.

- *Gracias Senor Alphonso.*
- *Muchas gracias, dona Solenne. Muchas gracias.*

Solenne and John walk slowly in a small alley and exchange their impressions on the people, on their way of life and the relaxed and harmonious ways.

John and Solenne had been walking for at least fifteen minutes when they decided to go see Leopold. A chariot had been following them for some time now and Solenne turns to get the driver's attention.

- *Ola. Perdone.*
- *Si Senora.*
- *Puede conduciros en la casa del senor Maddock ? Conoce el senor Maddock?*
- *Si, si. Nosotros decemos "Don Leopoldo".*
- *Por favor ?*

Solenne and John get onboard the chariot and Solenne gives the driver the directions to Leopold's oasis.

They head deeper into the countryside and John admires, with awe, the different plantations of oranges, bananas and of vegetables.

The fruits here appear to grow without any human intervention. Everything overflows of freshness and the quantities are impressionable.

A little ways further, as they head down a small dirt road lined with palm trees and coconut trees, John and Solenne contemplate what surrounds them and take in all the energy they can.

With their eyes closed and relaxed, John and Solenne let themselves be cradled by the sound of the horse and of the deaf orders given by the driver.

Deep within their daydreaming, they are finally brought back by the driver's voice.

- *La casa de don Leopoldo senora.*

Having understood that they had arrived, Solenne thanks the driver and gives him his due.

They then descend the chariot and observe the fairytale like scenery.

They observed this magnificent clearing covered with sunshine, situated in the middle of the woods, bordered by generously covered trees, and then a small house located in the background with, at its side, a limpid and calm stream of water.

By the great number of birds present, this appeared to be a place where all the birds of the forest seamed to gather. Their singing united in one enjoyable harmony.

Solenne suddenly becomes nervous and indicates for John to advance.

- *Come on, lets go John.* States Solenne by having him take the advance.

John is quite surprised of this attitude and comments.

- *What's happening with you, you seem so nervous Solenne?*
- *No, come on. Keep going.*

John smiles and attempts to tease Solenne.

- *Would you happen to have a crush on that guy Solenne?*

Somewhat embarrassed, Solenne attempt to deny what was quite evident.

- *Don't be foolish John. As if I would get myself caught up with a guy that is ten years older than I!*

John new very well that this argument had no value but, out of politeness, he contented himself to keep his smile and to begin advancing.

As he was about to knock at the door, a soft and warm voice
addressed them from afar.

•   *Well, whom do I owe the honors of such a visit?*

John and Solenne turn around and observe Leopold approaching
towards them. He was returning from the forest and was holding a bun-
dle of plants in his hands.

Leopold was an elegant man of sixty-five years of age. His athletic
appearance and the strength of his look would not give him more
than thirty.

Dressed in white and with his "salt and pepper hair, Leopold looked
like a God. His thick eyebrows gave an even greater contrast to his face
from which appeared to be escaping a bright light. His well-trimmed
beard fit in perfectly with the rest and having gone white with the years,
blended in very well with his attire.

Having approached a bit, Leopold salutes them with his hand and
keeps approaching.

•   *Hello Solenne. Pleased to see you again.* Simply states Leopold.

Solenne is shocked by his relaxed attitude and so candid which only
shows his perfect domination over his sentiments. But, she also knows
very well that she cannot hide her feelings and that nothing can fool
this man.

•   *We were just passing through and I got this great idea...*Replies
    Solenne in one breath.

To once again tease his sister, John whispers the following.

- *Exactly, we were just passing by…we went out this morning to buy some bread and…without knowing how…here we are…it's crazy how we can sometimes get too distracted…*

Obviously bothered by this, Solenne turns towards John, while Leopold is still approaching, and indicates to him that it is enough.
Leopold finally arrives and begins.

- *I'm quite pleased to see you Solenne. Actually, I was just thinking of you a little earlier. I knew that you would come. Aren't those agents some difficult!*
- *How to think otherwise.* Continued Solenne.
- *And this brave man Solenne, would this not be you wonderful brother you have told me so much about?*
- *Actually yes. This is John. John, this is Leopold.*
- *Pleased to meet you Mr Maddock.* States John not too certain what to think anymore.
- *Encantando John!*

John had noticed that Leopold appeared to know what had shaken them at the airport but believed he may just be quite familiar with the customs' procedures and that this probably happened quite frequently.

- *I've heard so much about you John. I have the impression that we have never been strangers. What do you think?*

Without really grasping the depth of this remark, John clumsily answers.

- *My sister's friends are my friends…*

Solenne lowers her eyes for, knowing Leopold very well, she new what he was really attempting to do.

- *Come; let's enter a while. I have to simmer these plants. You can taste it later, you'll see, you will love it.*

Thirteenth Chapter

Comfortably seated in armchairs and placed in a circle around a coffee table, John Solenne and Leopold get better acquainted.

John finally passes the remark that this place pleases him and that he sees a certain analogy with the one he had seen in his dream the night before.

- *It's true, aside the space ships that we have not yet encountered, the resemblance is remarkable.*

Leopold smiles and acknowledged with a head tilt.

- *That must mean something John.* Continues Leopold.
- *If I dared express myself, I would say…*
- *Go on, say it John.* Interrupts Solenne.
- *You guys will find this dumb but…*
- *No, not at all. Nothing else could interest us more.* Confirms Leopold.
- *Well, here it is. For the past few months I feel as though I'm caught up in an evolutional courant. Almost as though at times I feel I'm losing control. But at the en, I realize that I can only follow it.*

- *Since I've arrived in LA, ten days ago, this motion has become stronger and I have lived so many instructive situations to the point where I thought I was going to lose my mind. I had so much trouble keeping up with it. There were even a few times when I've told myself "That's it, I've become crazy". I honestly believed being disconnected from reality. If someone had followed me, they would have immediately referred me to a psychiatrist. On the other hand, now, bit-by-bit, I'm beginning to assimilate all the lessons that I have learned by experiences lived under the tutoring of a well-informed person.*

John then turns towards Solenne confirming the tutor he had mentioned.

- *What, as though everything had been decided in advance John?* Continues Solenne naively.
- *Continue John; I believe we are getting somewhere.* States Leopold.
- *Okay, where was I...*
- *...Assimilating the experiences.* States Leopold.
- *Ah yes! I knew I was learning something big. I realized that Solenne was guiding me but her play was so delicate that I believed I was discovering everything at the same time as her. That is what encouraged me to continue.*
- *Most definitely* interrupts Leopold, *because if we feel the other is too far ahead it creates a great distance, we lose courage, it has us believing we will never reach that level. Some people even attempt to pull back those who they feel are much more ahead than them.*
- *Only, correct me if I'm wrong Solenne, these last twenty-four hours I feel I have reached a peak. I felt a slowing down on Solenne's part, as though she was letting me know, without words; "As of this moment, it's every man for himself".*
- *And how did that make you feel?* Questions Leopold.

- *I didn't tell her of course but I was afraid to, once again, find myself alone and not be able to move forward, I was even afraid of going backwards, to fall…*

To these words, John remains still and appears to be searching deep within his memory.

- *What's wrong John? Asks Solenne.*
- *Nothing…it's only that…I just remembered a dream.*
- *What dream would that be? Continues Solenne.*
- *I told you about it…it's the one where I accompany Simeon in a ski resort and where I then join you.*
- *Yeah, I remember.*
- *We then found ourselves in a construction site. Continues John.*
- *And what happened in that place. Asks Leopold quite intrigued.*
- *I had to keep advancing in spite of the threats or my fears.*
- *You now know, John. Answers Leopold.*
- *Yes, I clearly understand.*

John begins laughing.

- *It's crazy what a dream can signify. Continues John.*
- *What exactly are you referring to? Asks Leopold.*
- *To the construction site.*

Then John lets out two or three more giggles.

- *What else did I have to build but myself? Poor idiot. How cold I have not thought about it before?*

Solenne and Leopold join John in his laughter.

- *And after the construction site, what else was there in this dream John? Asks Leopold.*
- *Solenne told me that I had to go with her…on a mountain…no, but this can't be.*

Leopold observes John and continues.

- *Give a speech, attend a course, finish a drawing…what was it John?*
- *That's it. That's exactly it. Give a speech. But how…*

John appears to now realize that he is sitting in front of a very real mystical character. He understands the power held by a person who is enlightened.

Embarrassed and confused by his impertinence, John mechanically glances at his watch to somewhat occupy himself.

- *This watch is finished. The needles are going crazy.*
- *Don't worry about it.* States Leopold. *It will become normal once you leave this place.*
- *What is this place, a magnetic field or what?* Asks John.
- *Something of the sort. Did you not notice that there are no electronic appliances here?* Casually ask Leopold.
- *And why is that?* Continues John.

Leopold gets up to get the herbal tea he had prepared with his plants and addresses Solenne.

- *Explain it to him Solenne, I will get the tea.*

Solenne gets closer to John and talks in a very low voice.

- *Leopold has attained a level of vibration so elevated that he can only surround himself with elements capable of supporting such energy.*
- *Like the trees, the forest?* Continues John.
- *That's correct. To live in the city would cause him great problems and people would also cause him trouble. No electronic appliances can remain insensitive in his presence.*

John once again glances at his watch and realizes that it is still under this magic even though Leopold is in another room

- *Wonderful. This means that his subtle bodies have reached a peak, that if he were to go further...*
- *He would disappear John. I even doubt that he attempted such an experience.*
Continues Solenne in an even lower tone of voice.
- *If a simple watch reacts, how could our physical bodies not react to this?*
- *Well brother, we react to influences of the sun, the moon...we have our own energetic fields. By amplifying them we make our own bodies react. We even sometimes get ill, therefore, why not react in a reverse sense...*

John turns and glances outside. Surprised, he observes Leopold calmly walking at about fifty meters from the house.

- *But...what is he doing outside?*

Stunned, John touches Solenne to direct her attention towards what is taking place outside.
Solenne turns around but as she looks in that direction, Leopold is no longer there.

- *Where?* Ask Solenne.

- *I'm telling you, he was there just a moment ago!* Exclaims John.

On these words Leopold does his entrance into the living room with a serving of tea.

- *Where you talking to me John?* Asks Leopold.

John appears troubled, even bothered and addresses Leopold in one breath of air.

- *Listen, I don't know who you are, what you want from me nor what you are doing to my sister, but I don't find it amusing the way you are mocking us. What was that by the way, a holographic trick or some cinema graphic magic…I just saw you outside, not even ten seconds ago, don't tell me I was dreaming…*

Leopold lays the tea service on the table and answers John in a calm and serine tone of voice and a smile.

- *You had fun with a stewardess on the plane, John. Did you not enjoy it?*

Even more surprised by the fact that Leopold is aware of this detail, John feels forced to admit.

- *Of course but…I didn't do it on purpose…* states John.
- *Fortunately. It was an accident. But for that poor young woman, don't you believe that it would have been better that she not know?* Continues Leopold.

John agrees, somewhat sheepish, basically defeated.

- *You're right. But there…how do you…*

Solenne, who silently observed the entire scene understood that Leopold just gave a demonstration to John and that this demonstration carried, in itself, a very important message.

- *John, I believe Leopold has something very important to tell us. He did not want to frighten you. Tell me if I'm mistaken Leopold, but I believe you just wanted to teach us a lesson.*

Leopold takes a sip of his soothing liquid and adds.

- *You know a lot of things now John. You are at the point of no return. The first rule you must remember was that one.*
- *That it is not a game.* Continues John somewhat defeated.
- *That's correct. Do what you have to but don't bother anyone with it. Join the great white universal fraternity but do not impose these laws upon those who are not yet ready. Remain deaf, dumb and blind. Especially, do not provoke! Be wise in the way you use your new powers. The time has not yet come to expose them in broad daylight. We are an insufficient number. This could create social disorder, religious, economic or even family and they would be beyond repair. Content yourself in just "being there", right Solenne?* Concludes Leopold while winking amusingly to Solenne.

John looks at Solenne, Solenne looks at John and they are both thinking the same thing.

How, once again, could Leopold have used the exact same expression that Solenne gave John upon his arrival in LA.

- *Who are you…or should I say what?* Ask John, having returned to his role of questioner. *How could you know everything? You had us followed, is that it?*

Pretending to not have understood, Leopold requests John to be more precise.

- *It's as though you had me followed since I've left Quebec. You know certain details that no one could simply guess.*

Leopold sets his cup down and kindly looks at John.

- *As I, you will have to sponsor someone else. With the new powers that you will soon acquire, you will be capable to succeed at your tasking but remember, you will have to act parsimoniously. You will learn on your own, you'll see, it's very simple after all.* Continues Leopold.
- *You mean to say that I was…*
- *My protégé.* Replies Leopold.
- *But what about Solenne?* Wonders John out loud.
- *She was your accompanist.*

John then realizes that nothing was a coincidence. His entire life appeared having been traced in advance. All of a sudden, he realizes that all he could have done would have only delayed his process.

Suddenly, he sees himself back in prison, he sees himself isolated in his house in St-Cecile and his reaction clearly shows on his face.

Leopold finally reassures him.

- *We don't all understand at the same speed John, but the important thing is to understand. You did not do all that for nothing. But it is important that you understand that once you have left this evolutional stagnation, you must go forward, always forward. Boy did you ever take you sweet old time but once you decided to go…(Leopold laughs and looks at Solenne) you needed someone to drive, or else…*

John regains his senses and continues his interrogation, determined, this time, to take another step forward.

- *Forgive me Solenne…I was here but had not yet arrived.*

Solenne and Leopold burst out laughing and finally feel relieved.

- *Good, finally, welcome to the white universal fraternity John.* Continues Leopold.

John gets up and clowns around as he does a sign of reverence

- *Seriously Leopold…am I also going to disappear? Asks John.*
- *You will be able to; soon…you only have to learn to concentrate, to meditate properly, to develop certain breathing techniques and to find the exit door.*
- *There's an exit door? Asks John curiously.*

At this moment Solenne becomes as intrigued as John.

- *The door that brings us to the other world? Asks Solenne.*
- *Yes.*
- *The one that is mentioned in this last book you had me read?* Continues Solenne.
- *Exactly. Replies Leopold.*
- *What book are you talking about? Interrupts John attempting to* reenter the conversation.
- *Oh, a book that describes in some sort, certain powers not yet explored by mankind. Replies Leopold.*

• *It takes place somewhere in the Andes.* Continues Solenne.

They continued the remainder of their day harmoniously by visiting the sites and the various strong energetic points. Leopold made surprising revelations to Solenne and John.

Several subjects were discussed; medicine, religions, science, politics, the vanished populations as the Incas, the Mayas, the Aztecs, this other Mexican Totonak ancestral population; the el Tahin in the region of Vera Cruz, the secrets of Atlantis, the life beyond, the destiny of mankind, the roles played by the great biblical figures, and the popular subjects such as marriage, sexuality from every angle including homosexuality, inter-personal relations, and Leopold also taught them what their respective roles would be in the new society that should immerge soon.

John and Solenne then realized that their path was really a long preparatory period for an ultimate mission.

Once the night arrived, Leopold invited them to stay for the night and to share breakfast with him the following morning.

John and Solenne quickly accepted without any hesitation.

The following morning they enjoyed this breakfast outdoors and discussed how each of them had arrived to this point in life.

John remembered his dream where he arrived at this place by a different trail then Solenne.

He mentions this to Leopold and also adds that he understands that everyone uses a different trail that is unique to him but that at the end, we should all arrive at the same place, the quicker the better but that no steps were to be missed.

After breakfast, Leopold accompanied them down the dirt road that would bring them back home.

John first hesitated but then commented.

- *We would need someone to take us back; we cannot do all this traveling by foot.*

Leopold just looks at him and waits to see what John will decide.
Then forgetting this last detail, John takes a stupefied look and confides.

- *I think I know where the exit door is! I received the answer last night. My dream appeared to be connected to this, now I only have to decipher it...*

Leopold remains inert and waits.
John continues.

- *And you Solenne, do you have a clue about it?*
- *I believe I may have found it too...I believe...*
- *I woke up with a very strong intuition this morning...but I prefer to not share it with you for the moment, if you understand?*

Solenne and John look at each other and John concludes.

- *But that does not bring a solution to our present locomotive problem...*states John...*nonetheless, I feel that I should not worry about it...I don't know why but I feel that this problem is already taken care of.*
- *I also feel that way.* Continues Solenne.
- *Yet...I don't see anything ahead...weird.* Comments John.

Leopold looks at them, amused, and as he is about to answer them, the sound of a chariot can be heard from a distance.

- *See Leopold, I told you so. Not bad for a new enlightened.*

Solenne lowers her head and humbly answers.

• *If we would have felt this last night we would have understood your insistence in our remaining here master Leopold.*

Leopold looks at Solenne and smiles.

• *I knew that your passing was short but I also knew that another person was ready to arrive. I was warned. But don't worry, you may leave in peace. Leonardo will take you. It must have been him who warned me last night.*

John remains amazed.

• *Ah!…because Leonardo is…*
• *Evidently John…*
• *Yesterday, when he followed us with his chariot…*
• *Yes, he knew!* Concluded Leopold.

John is still quite amazed. He approaches the chariot and a woman of a certain age descends giving way for John and Solenne to board.
Leopold greets the woman and salutes John and Solenne.
Some ways away, John turns around and asks very loudly to Leopold.

• *Mr Maddock, how will I recognize my protégé?*

From afar, we see that Leopold understood John's question but he simply turns around and continues to walk away with his future enlightened.
In the chariot, John addresses Solenne.

• *I think he didn't hear me.*

At that same moment, John finds himself thinking of Simeon.

Simeon had not once been on his mind and now, as he asks this question, he finds Simeon's image occupying his entire thoughts as though he were haunting him.

- *I just got the answer Solenne. This jerk answered me without even saying a word. This Leopold is some powerful. I will come back to see him some day.*

Solenne and John leave quite enchanted with their trip and return to Los Angeles by that afternoon.

Fourteenth Chapter

The following two weeks were spent with John and Solenne exchanging their thoughts on this world of energetic forces and the multiple possibilities in which it can be used.

With all of this new information John felt transformed, he had the impression of being reborn. A new life was opening before him. John was departing with a suitcase twice as heavy.

On the day of his departure, John took one last moment to admire the view from the living room.

He was standing in front of the window in a religious contemplation.

Solenne was behind him, seated and reading a book and a soft music could be heard playing in the background.

- *He's going to die.* Suddenly states John.
- *Excuse me?* Replies Solenne.
- *That tree…it's going to die.*
- *But what makes you say such a thing John?*
- *Look, haven't you ever notices that tree over there. You must intervene quickly or else it will die Solenne.*

Solenne takes this seriously and gets up to join John.

- *What tree are you talking about John?*
- *That one there, just in front.*
- *The big one?*
- *No, the other next to it, the small one Solenne.*
- *But it appears healthy John. It even has all its leaves. And the gardener has not mentioned anything to me in that regards.*
- *But I'm telling you Solenne; it is showing signs of weakness.*
- *How do you know that?*

John remains inert in front of this window, with a frantic look on his face and stares at the tree in question.

- *A gray cloud…* continues John.
- *Where?*
- *Around it, all around it.* Replies John. *The others are trying to help it but the problem appears to be coming from the roots. You have to air out the ground, I don't really know what exactly but the problem is quite deep. If we don't do anything about it this tree will be dried up by next year.*

Solenne immediately understood that John was once again seeing auras. All living things, no matter what it is, releases energy and therefore possesses an aura, even the vegetation. Solenne new this very well but she had not yet developed this gift

- *If you see a gray cloud releasing itself from this tree, then it's certain that it is sick.*
Continues Solenne.
- *Not only do I see this gray cloud but I also see very dense white courant leaving the other trees nearby and that are going straight to*

this sick tree. They are trying to help but they are weakening them-selves and will be affected if nothing is done.
- *You say it has to do with its roots John?*
- *Yes that's it, the roots. Something has happened to them recently. I say that it is recent because the energetic loss is quick and is still in movement,...and also, the exterior signs have not begun showing. The gray cloud comes from the ground...*

Solenne reflects on this and finally agrees with John.

- *But of course. Exclaims Solenne. I know what it is. The asphalt of our street was redone not long ago and they had to dig to install a new sewer system. Actually, it was exactly there that they dug. They must have cut a main root of the tree to install the piping.*
- *Well my dear Solenne...your tree is gong to die. You must cut it down or it will take others along with it.*

After a moment of silence and daydreaming, John regains his senses and regrets that he is leaving a place that teaches him so much.

- *We have to go Solenne. My flight is in two hours. I'd love to stay but I feel I need to absorb all of this and the country air is just the place for that.*

On their way to the airport John and Solenne review the events of their past two weeks and John, once again, tells of his dream where he saw himself with Solenne in the ski resort and where he had also aban-doned Simeon.

- *You see Solenne, I've just learned another thing form our dreams, they are often there to help us accept what is going to happen to us. Of course the dream precedes the event but I would have never guessed that this particular dream would have anything to do with my trip to Los Angeles.*

- *One day John you will be able to decipher your dreams in advance and that will permit you to live the events with all the serenity possible. Eventually, it may be possible for you to use this power to help others, to heal them, to warn them of possible danger but nevertheless, by still respecting the natural order.*
- *I now know Solenne that there is at least you who understands me.*
- *Why do you say that John?*
- *Oh, I talked a bit about this with Simeon but I think I lost him.*
- *Simeon is not at a level to be able to accept these things yet John. Let him go at his own speed. You noticed that even at the level where we are at, Leopold was able to confuse us.*
- *That is exactly what I told myself. But now I understand that I must follow with Simeon without pushing him. I know what it is I have to do. Therefore, my encounter with Leopold had two goals; perfecting my path and to prepare myself to help another.*
- *Remember John, there are things we must not change, it could ruin everything; remember the billiard effect.*
- *Yes I know, in other words, to relieve suffering is not always possible.*
- *That's correct. Suffering is an institution in itself.*

Finally arrived at the airport, Solenne accompanies John towards the boarding gate.

As they were walking along, John notices a person not too far away which causes him to immediately stop.

- *What's wrong John?*
- *That woman…*
- *Which woman?* Questions Solenne.
- *The woman from the plane, the one that had the gray cloud above her left breast, that's her over there.*

- *Do you still see the cloud?*
- *No, of course not Solenne, I must be too…awake, too much into the physical reality, but it is definitely her.*
- *Lets go meet her and see where it leads us.* Continues Solenne.
- *But I really don't want to…*
- *Let things happen as they go along. If she was once again put on our path, it's that we must go see her. She might have something to teach us.*

John follows Solenne who has picked up the pace in the direction of this woman.

As they arrive next to her, the woman turns and speaks to her husband.

- *I'm going to buy the newspaper before boarding dear.*

Then as she turns and faces Solenne and John, she recognizes John.

- *Excuse me Sir, but aren't you from Montreal?* Asks the woman.

Nervously, John replies.

- *Yes, we were on the same flight over.*
- *We are also leaving this morning.* Comments the woman.
- *Two weeks, it makes for quite a short trip.* Continues John in an attempt to keep the conversation going.
- *Oh, we were supposed to be here for the summer. I have a sister who lives here but a small hitch is forcing us to return home.*
- *Nothing serious I hope?* Continues John innocently.

Solenne remains somewhat aside from them and smiles at John. She is making a few faces to tease him. She also attempts to remind him the "cloud" in a way that embarrasses him.

The woman notices that John's concentration is elsewhere and looks behind to see what it is but at the same time continues her conversation without stopping to breath.

- *Well actually, believe it or not I had a small discomfort three days ago, a small cramp in the thorax area. My husband keeps saying that I eat too much but I never listen to him. You know what I mean.*

The woman's husband listens without tiring and simply acknowledges by yes or no with a head gesture, as would a wise and well -trained dog.

John appears bored by this woman who is a little too ordinary and he looks for a way out but untiring, the woman continues.

- *And as I was about to find a place by the hotel pool,…oh I'm not saying that there weren't any good looking young men there, ha ha ha…then I felt my two legs give way and the next thing I remember is looking up and seeing the face of this sweet nurse who was taking my pressure.*
- *And finally, what was it?* Asks John in an attempt to conclude this extremely boring conversation.
- *A very small heart attack. They said that one of my heart vessels is on the verge of becoming obstructed and that it had to be taken care of immediately. Right George?*

George, her husband, had no choice but to acknowledge with a head tilt once again.

- *Luckily the insurance company covered everything but we were told that we had to immediately return to Quebec to receive further and more thorough treatments. Here, they don't have a medical plan as we do at home and I'm pretty sure that a cardiac bypass must cost an arm and a leg.*

In a lower tone of voice, she confides to John.

• *George thinks that I fainted because of one of these handsome young men who didn't stop looking at me. I kept the secret, he has become so jealous.*

John timidly smiles but has trouble believing that the good old George could show jealousy for such a boring and not too good looking nag. And that a young man could have actually showed interest but finally, he had the answer he was looking for. But now he was stuck with another problem and did not quite know how to get out o fit.

Luckily, Solenne was there to intervene.

• *John, we must hurry.* Interrupts Solenne.
• *I'm coming Solenne, I'll be right there.*
• *Is she your wife?* Asks the woman.
• *Well...Yeah...* Replies John feeling somewhat trapped.
• *She is very lovely...you should not have her wait like this...you talk too much. Go on, we'll see each other on the plane.*

Finally free, John joins Solenne.

• *Ah, that woman!* Exclaims John.
• *Too bad she's married John.* Comments Solenne mockingly.
• *Too bad for her husband, I agree!*

As John lifts his heavy suitcase he feels a sharp pain in his back and immediately stops moving.

- *What's wrong John?* Ask Solenne worried.

John remains silent, regains his breath and then attempts to reassure Solenne.

- *Oh, this pain in my back, it just came back.*
- *Have you seen a doctor John?*
- *Yes but he couldn't find anything.*

Solenne appears worried. John once again becomes silent and passes ahead of her. Solenne becomes more and more pensive and begins daydreaming. She remains there, questioning herself. Suddenly she experiences an event which she had always envied of John.

Her semi-cataleptic state enables her to perceive the invisible. She was fixed on John questioning herself in regards to this mysterious back pain and suddenly she could see John's aura.

It was exactly as John had described it. The colors were of a changing blue, with small purple currants, violets and indigo. She then notices a gray cloud on his left backside, just at the height of his thorax.

Stupefied she interrupts John.

- *John…John, stop!* Exclaims Solenne.
- *What's wrong Solenne?* Asks John as he turns around to face her.
- *You definitely have something wrong.*
- *But I already told you Solenne…*
- *No, I just saw it, a second ago.*
- *What exactly did you see Solenne?*
- *A cloud…a gray cloud…right there.* Continues Solenne as she indicates the area on his back.

John appears worried but attempts to render the situation somewhat unimportant.

- *I was actually just asking myself what I had given you in the past two weeks. You were finally able to se an aura Solenne.*
- *It's not funny John. You have to have this checked out. See a specialist if necessary.*

Having arrived at the boarding entrance, John had to leave Solenne.

- *I'll see to it Solenne, don't worry about anything.*
- *I'll go see Leopold. He will tell me how to remove what it is you are suffering from.*
- *I'll be fine Solenne, trust me. I'll keep you posted.*

John and Solenne bid farewell and John leaves for Montreal with two extra manuscripts in his infamous suitcase.

Once onboard the plane, John reviews the strong sensations he has lived in the past fourteen days and feel great satisfaction.

In a clumsy gesture, the man seated next to John slightly hits John while attempting to pick up a book he wanted to read.

John politely moves to give the man some room to maneuver and then once seated properly, the man thanks him and attempts a discussion with him.

- *I've recently began reading this book. Have you heard of it?*

The young man, who appears to be in his thirties, holds out the book in question. John recognizes the title and author.

- *Of course. I have not yet had the pleasure to read it but my sister, whom I have been visiting with, told me about it. Actually, she strongly recommended it.* Replies John.

- *You might not like it. It's based purely on fiction except that there are some allusions of extraordinary revelations that are quite interesting.. I'm already at the sixth one.*
- *Oh you know young man…one must keep an open mind. The line that separates fiction from reality is sometimes quite thin.*

The young man feels that John is beating around the bush and so he decides to get to the point.

- *You are one of them, aren't you?* Asks the young man.
- *What exactly are you talking about, one of what?* Asks John.
- *No, nothing, I…*

Uncomfortable, the young man finds refuge in his book but then John attempts to hide the effect of surprise that almost revealed him.

- *You must be talking about an adept in actual theories and of the very popular spiritual fulfillment.* Comments John.

The young man immediately returns to the conversation and continues.

- *Yes, that's it. Don't you find that we are heading into an era where people are turning more and more towards their inner selves?*
- *Yes,* replies John. *They are searching for new truths, new land. Exploring new frontiers is part of the human nature but at this moment, people attempt to search for the new destinations within themselves. It's actually a very good thing.*
- *There is a chapter in this book,* continues the young man, *where it is implied that one day it would be possible to know everything by having access to the universal knowledge. Do you know what they mean by that?*

John attempts to answer by pretending to use logical reasoning and simple deduction.

- *In my opinion...I believe that...I believe that what they mean must be that there is another way of being that is coming than an acute possibility of intellectual faculties.*
- *A way of being?* Asks the young man.
- *Yes, I suppose by this that a true genius does not really exist.*
- *But come on sir, how could you explain all the great ones such as Mozart, Einstein, Galilee, Edison, the Wright's brothers, Alexander Graham Bell, Beethoven, and I'm skipping some, aren't they geniuses still recognized to this date in their respective fields?*

- *Looked at it in this way, of course. But If we had to wait for a genius to manifest himself before we could make a step forward, in this physical world, we would still have to wait another two thousand years before reaching a point where life would become more tolerable.* Exclaims John.
- *But how would you qualify these people who have made humanity take giant steps forward?*
- *I don't know.* Replies John. *Probably just the fact that they are very receptive people, those that their faculties permit them to have access to the universal knowledge. If we admitted that it is possible for this to exist of course!*
- *Which would mean that these people have only taken information which already exists somewhere?*
- *In some way, yes.* Continues John. *The universal science, the universal knowledge, call it what you want, would be a place, still unknown, where everything already exists.*
- *By developing certain faculties, we can have access to it and by doing this we can bring forward information leading to the elaboration of new elements which were, up until then, non-existing.*

- *Your stuff really makes sense.* Exclaims the young man.
- *Otherwise,* continues John. *We would not know any more about the phone than we did three hundred years ago.*
- *I don't quite follow you sir.*
- *What I mean is that, for example, lets take a thousand years ago, the possibility to communicate by wires or satellite already existed. But nobody, at that time, could connect themselves to the fact that by uniting elements present in nature, it would give birth to the telephone as well as the automobile or light.*
- *It is hard to deny that one.* Replies the young man.
- *Evidently. Everything that is given to us through technology and science already existed since the beginning of time. But it is only on a gradual term that these elements were materialized.*
- *According to you, we only materialize, that is to render denser, what already exists at a more subtle state?* Asks the young man.
- *Exactly, my theory is quite simple.* Replies John. *It's no better than any other one.*
- *But why does everything appear to evolve with a certain chronological order? Why is it, otherwise put, that we didn't invent, what is it called…nuclear propulsion before the mechanical propulsion if both already existed? Why spend so many years pushing a chariot when the possibility of traveling at the speed of sound already existed, somewhere in the clouds?*
- *By pure respect of the universal laws.* Replies John.
- *These famous universal laws, do you know what they are all about?* Further questions the young man.
- *I have a vague idea.*

John felt that the young man was on the right path but he remembered Leopold's advise. " Do not frighten, remain at the other person's level. To attract them is far better than to scare them off; we have less resistance that way."

- *I believe that it is also a matter of evolution.* Continues John Mankind, *although he is quite easily adaptable, can only take from the universal laws what he is capable of receiving at that moment.*
- *I have trouble understanding what you just said.*
- *It's simple,* replies John. *Give a very powerful car to a five-year-old child. He won't even be able to move it one inch. Give him a tricycle and he will be able to go where he wants. Later on in life, give him the car again and this time he will go further and faster. In the same line of thought, the more mankind evolves, the quicker he advances but one day he must reach a peak and continue his path by retrieving from another sphere of knowledge. Otherwise put, his intellect must gradually adapt itself to the new realities before conceiving more advanced structures. Man's spirit must wait until his intellect reaches a superior level before it can manifest itself further, as though the intellect is very slow in reacting. The day where our intellect will be subordinated, passed, almost ignored and that we will almost exclusively use our superior senses, science will evolve at a speed which will make us dizzy, it will be staggering.*
- *But if I were to give the car to a ten year old, wouldn't he be able to use it? He would eventually find the contact key and the shifting gear...*
- *By also placing himself in a position of extreme danger.* Interrupts John. *He could destroy himself and his environment.*
- *If you possess the control of a faucet from which flows the good things you must permit your child, you will present him these things gradually so that he may tame them one by one, according to his wisdom and maturity.*

- *But what if my child one day loses his head and uses these things to harm...*
- *Won't you take it away from him?!* Concludes John.

The young man is very pleased with this conversation and expresses it to John.

- *You are so wise sir. I finally believe that you will find this book quite ordinary.*
- *We always have something to learn.* Comments John.
- *Then it is to be understood that Mozart and all the others only deserve the merit of having succeeded in connecting themselves, a the right moment.*
- *Correct.* Replies John. *It proves that these people had access to this everlasting source of knowledge and, therefore, are not equipped with a great uncommon intelligence, but with an ultra-sensitive receptivity. In their time, they brought the elements in which mankind required at this level of evolution. Finally, they were simple channels through which traveled the elements that mankind needed. They have but the merit of being highly evolved people for their time, which is not to be belittled, believe me. Those people have somewhat suffered from their advance state of mind.*
- *But if we had evaluated these people's intellectual quotient, they would have certainly obtained fantastic results. Doesn't this prove that intelligence has its role to play?* Asks the young man.
- *Let me answer you by ways of image. Imagine a person so pure that he instantly has access to this unlimited reserve of knowledge. We have him undergo psychometric evaluation tests. You can very well imagine that the results would foil all present scientific understanding. We would no longer be talking about a genius but of a...God. I believe that when we evaluate a person, we really only evaluate the level of open mind of this person. The brain is nothing more than an*

intermediate used to idealize and transmit information coming from a much higher level. The brain is but the link between this source of information and the physical world in which we live. It analyzes, idealize, concretizes…but it creates…nothing. For me, the intellect has no other use than to do our end of the month bills, dumb stuff of the sort. When I'm searching for a solution to a real problem, I refer to other faculties, subtler, more certain.

- *You mean using your intuition?* Asks the young man quite intrigued.
- *Yes, that's it,* replies John.

John then smiles to the young man and as though to amuse himself, he signals the man to be quiet, as though someone could overhear them.

The young man appears amused by this gesture and giggles.

John then sinks comfortably in his seat and concludes this contact by a simple friendly wink of an eye to the young man.

Proud and completely overjoyed, this young man opens his book and continues his reading with great interest.

Fifteenth Chapter

Once landed in Montreal John awaits Simeon who is to give him a ride home.

Here he is, finally glad to see his brother.

- *Hi John, nice trip?*
- *Oh just wonderful. I would even say enriching.* Replies John.

Simeon helps John put his suitcase in the truck and then they take the road home.

They held a few exchanges of second nature in regards to John's trip in the city, the people there and Solenne's family situation. Afterwards Simeon opens the conversation towards that which he really wanted to discuss.

- *You know what John, certain things have happened since you left.*
- *Oh yeah?*
- *Yes. I extensively questioned myself. I had mentioned to you that my life appeared*

- *wanting to take a new direction after you had shared your personal research with me.*
- *Yes Simeon. I remember this very well.*
- *I sort of found myself in front of a black whole. I looked back on everything I succeeded and it appeared as though I was totally forgetting myself.*
- *Which means…*
- *Well John, that did not bring me much satisfaction to own all the land of the village, as a nobody, I couldn't get to know my true value.*
- *Well this is amazing Simeon, you are becoming quite spiritual.*

Simeon becomes somewhat shy but also flattered by this remark.

- *So then I began making an assessment of my own values. Well, I realized that I'm not such a bad guy after all, I'm kind with people, considerate, I have patience…but all that still left me somewhat empty.*
- *Yet they are great qualities that represent you well Simeon. Isn't this enough to value ourselves?* Asks John innocently.
- *Yes I know. I'm probably not expressing myself properly. But, it appears to me that all of a sudden taking all my qualities and faults, of course, did not fill this emptiness I felt. I had the impression that there was still something missing, I could say that through everything I was doing, everything I was being, I couldn't manage to express myself.*

John was quite anxious to know what was going to immerge from this preamble but kept this detached attitude.

- *And so, tell me what happened that was so extra-ordinary.* Requests John.

- *Extra-ordinary, I don't' know but something that really surprised Rachel.*
- *And what was it Simeon?*
- *Do you remember the old Canadian accordion that dad bought when we were children?*
- *Of course I remember. I especially remember how well you played it Simeon. You could have become a great folks musician.*

- *Well imagine this. After all those years of not even touching it, I recently took it out and began playing again.*

Acting innocent John then adds.

- *If nothing more, an accordion can sure bring entertainment in someone's life.*
- *But I'm telling you John,* states Simeon quite encouraged. *When I'm playing music, I have the impression of escaping, of being somewhere else, of becoming someone else.*

John feels he hit the nail on the head, so to speak. He could see in Simeon's phrases the path he was beginning to take towards the universal fraternity. Each individual takes the path best suited for him, had commented Leopold.

John then resumed in attempting to be precise as the impressions that Simeon felt.

- *I think I understand Simeon You are more than likely trying to tell me that you express a part of yourself which is trying to express itself by the vehicle of music.*
- *Yes that's it, exactly it John. It fills me. When I'm playing I feel powerful, I feel very light and filled with energy.....I love my work, my family but I only feel these impressions when I'm playing my music.*

- *That's good. Its very good Simeon. Keep playing; don't stop, for as long as you have these feelings.*

Simeon stares at the road ahead and becomes pensive.

- *Tell me John. You seem to want to tell me something without really saying it.*

John first hesitates and then resumes.

- *It's very simple Simeon. You now know why you are here. Without a doubt you probably undertook what all individuals must do sooner or later.*
- *Explain this to me John.*
- *You are presently searching for your own identity. Through music, you have reached areas, that were unknown until now and when you reach this level, you have the impression that a whole new world opens up to you. It's somewhat as though you had discovered a new country and now you had to explore it.*
- *That's it, exactly it John.*

Simeon acknowledges the exactitude of John's word and then continues.

- *There is one problem though, Rachel is getting quite worried. She thinks I'm having a burn out or that the accordion is taking her place.*
- *It's normal Simeon. When we reach that level, we change a lot of our principles already established and those who surround us think we are losing it. All you have to do is reassure them, that it won't last but you must not ever quite.*
- *But she's almost demanding that I do quit.*

- *Give it time Simeon. She will have but one alternative; to join you or lose you; but you cannot and must not go backwards. Anyways, what's wrong with playing the accordion two or three hours a day; it's not as though you were going to a bar every night.*

Simeon reviews this short exchange and displays a look of satisfaction on his face. He feels supported, less isolated in his process. He seems to be giving himself just cause and determined to continue living what he had begun.

John and Simeon continued their discussions throughout their entire trip back and John very sparingly shared what he knew about this subject. He now realizes that Leopold saw clearly. Simeon was his protégé. It could not be any clearer.

He contented himself in simply answering Simeon's questions, existential questions that Simeon would not have even dared think a month prior.

John recognized his own path through Simeon, constantly questioning everything like a child who is discovering life.

John always provided answers which gave Simeon a choice but his answers directed this choice. Therefore Simeon believed he found the answers himself, which enforced his desire to continue his quest and Simeon couldn't feel the great distance which really separated him from John. This prevented Simeon from getting discouraged by being aware of the work he had left to do ahead.

Once arrived at his house, John thanked Simeon.

- *Thank you little brother. What would I do without you?*
- *Come over one of these nights John, we'll continue our conversation.*
- *It's a date; I'll call you Simeon.*

John entered his home just like a soldier returning from a victorious combat.

He put his manuscripts away and looked over the numerous notes he had taken throughout his trip.

Finally, exhausted by the traveling, John heads to bed.

For some time now he had stopped writing his dreams as though it were no longer important. He no longer kept his manuscript at his bedside either.

John was now aware that this period had been important but to continue writing his dreams would not help move further ahead.

But, that night John had a strong premonition dream. One of those dreams where you would prefer not remembering any of it when you awake, it was a real nightmare.

John finds himself in the desert, alone in this arid and flat scenery. He aimlessly strolls along and suddenly notices two men at the top of a very high mountain.

The rocky mountain is practically inaccessible to man and is highly erected in the center of this never-ending stretch of desert.

He approaches the two men who appear to be occupied to something common.

He places his two hands in front of his mouth to help carry his voice out to them.

- *Ohey…ohey…can you hear me?*

The two men do not react to John. He yells louder and louder, determined to get their attention.

- *Hey, you up there…can you hear me?*

Then, one of the men turns towards him. John has difficulty recognizing him but it really is him; it is his son Kevin. He then feels invaded by an uncontrollable fear, a horrible sensation invades him. He predicts that Kevin is in danger.

- *Come down Kevin, come down from there.*

Kevin does not answer.

- *Come down before it's too late Kevin.*

The other man then gets up. He becomes tall, very tall and John can now clearly see him. The strange and unpleasant man is dressed entirely in black with a gloomy and hideous face that resembles death.

John is frightened by this man. He fears that he is putting Kevin in great danger.

By the magic of dreams, John immediately transports himself to the summit and observes what was so interesting to Kevin and this black man.

They are finishing a game of chest. Kevin is playing with the white pieces and the other man with the black ones. It's Kevin's turn to play. He is stuck; his queen, his two towers and a majority of his pieces have disappeared. He only has one night and a few other pieces further away.

His king is in the open and the opponent has lost very few pieces.

Kevin feels this is a difficult game. John guesses the gloomy person's intentions.

Kevin prepares to move a piece but John intervenes;

- *No Kevin, no. You will be lost.*

Kevin looks at John and sheds a tear.

- *I don't have a choice, it's my turn, and I must play.*

Kevin is in a hopeless position with his King. No matter what he plays next, he will be lost.

In a last desperate attempt, Kevin wishes to put his opponent's king in a lost position so that he will then move under a threat without ever realizing that he, Kevin, is in a lost position.

- *You can quit everything Kevin. Just leave the game there where it is now.* Exclaims John.
- *But dad…*

The gloomy but lugubrious person begins laughing. He laughs so loud that his voice invades the entire desert and is amplified by the echo.

His gruesome laughter petrifies John and Kevin gets ready to touch his game piece.

- *No Kevin, don't. Don't do that. Don't play his game. Stop it, there's still time, leave that piece there, abandon your king Kevin.*

The gruesome man laughs even louder and invites Kevin to play;

- *Come Kevin, come closer, don't be afraid…you can't quit now…*

Then, Kevin finally touches the piece, moves it one set and the gloomy man yells very loudly with satisfaction and starts to get up from his seat.

- *CHECK MATE Kevin, you lose!!!!*

To these words the man gets up, flips the table over and Kevin stumbles, takes one step back and falls off the mountain. His fall takes him in a bottomless black pit.

John remains at the top feeling his soul destroyed. He looks at Kevin falling deeper into the whole and soon loses site of him and feels sad that he could not intervene.

John wakes up in a cold sweat, terrified and panicking. He wakes up crying heavily and is unable to contain it.

- *Kevin, Kevin.* Yells John alone in his home.

He looks at the time, it is five o'clock. John remains in shock. This dream had nothing good. Something is going to happen. Kevin is in danger, that's certain. John acknowledges that he ignored his dreams for too long but his time the impulse is too strong. It is not make belief. John knows that he must act.

He attempts to reason with himself and walks aimlessly throughout the house. An irresistible urge to call Kevin is eating him up inside. But at such an hour, he's going to be angry. But what if there really was something wrong, he could not live with it. John remembers the image of Mary during the accident that took her life, he relives his guilt. Then, the image of Kevin returns.

John cannot control himself; he does not know what to do. At the risk of passing for a mad man, he decides to follow his intuition.

- *No, not him. Not Kevin.* He keeps repeating to himself while clumsily dressing himself.

John rushes out of the house and heads for the stables. No Candy, she is still at Simeon's house.

There's no other choice. Run; run as fast as possible, without stopping.

John runs the entire way to Simeon's. For fifteen minutes John runs and attempts to remove this troubling premonition but reasoning gets involve and he cannot shake it. Once at Simeon's, he rushes to the stables to get Candy. He jumps on her back without any saddle, grabs the reins and flees for St Pierre.

Candy gallops the best she can and John encourages her.

- *Come Candy, come on girl, we're almost there. We'll make it.*

Candy gives her all as though she had felt the urgency of the situation. Nostrils dilated. Foam on her back, and once in a while grabbling some saliva with her tongue, Candy reaches the maximum speed worthy of a pure bred.

He finally arrives at Kevin's home. A pale light can be seen in the kitchen. John approaches the house.

At that moment he realizes that all of this was absurd. He is there, in front of the door, it's almost six in the morning, absolutely no life outside. He is there, frozen in front of his son's house, dressed haphazardly, breathless and excited. Candy remains behind not understanding her master's catastrophic return. Everything appears sleeping calmly inside. No danger in sight.

John then feels quite ridiculous and turns about. He is about to jump onto Candy when he suddenly hears Kevin;

- *What in God's name are you doing here at such an hour?* Questions Kevin through a half opened door and in a low voice.

John gently caresses Candy and ties her to a post. Then he comes towards Kevin while thinking about what he had to tell him. He felt the absurdity of this story but on the other hand his dream kept haunting him.

Let's cut to the chase, thinks John.

- *Listen Kevin. I don't care what you think about me and it will prob-ably get worst after I tell you what I have to say but who cares.*
- *What do you want exactly?*
- *I don't know what's new in your life or what you're working on but you must quit a project.*
- *What are you talking about dad?* Insists Kevin.
- *You're gambling with your life Kevin; you're gambling with your life. Stop it before it's too late.*
- *I'm sorry dad but this time you have gone overboard, you really lost it.*
- *I will have warned you. You'll see…*

Then John turns around and heads back to Candy.

- *Excuse me for having woken you.* Continues John, uncertain of himself and in a low tone of voice.
- *It's okay. I was already up. I was getting ready to leave.*

Standing with his back to Kevin, John becomes still, thinks a second and asks;

- *Where exactly are you going Kevin?*
- *What's it to you?*
- *Just tell me where it is you are going.* Asks John and once again turning towards Kevin.
- *I'm going with some friends; they will be here in an hour. You'll have to excuse me but I must get ready.*
- *Where are you guys going?* Asks John while taking a few steps towards Kevin.
- *Oh dad, please…. you're regressing my faith. I'm not five years old anymore.*
- *Just simply tell me where it is you are going and I will leave.*
- *We are going in the Eastern townships, are you satisfied?*

- *To do what exactly?*
- *We're going down a river, that's all, a guy thing. I need to get away and a friend suggested we go rafting down a turbulent river. The desire for strong emotions…I believe you know the feeling. Now I must go. You've really lost it dad.*
- *Don't go Kevin, forget these plans.*

Irritated by this behavior, Kevin slams the door and John remains abandoned not knowing what to think anymore.

- *Oh…what the hell, I will have warned him.*

Sixteenth Chapter

Three days have gone by and John withdrew to himself a little. No new incident has happened and there was no news of Kevin. No phone calls other the one from Solenne to whom John confided himself. He admitted having lost it but Solenne was not of the same advice. She told him to remain alert and to observe all new clues. But John took these encouraging words as simple moral comforting.

It is late and John feels having lost a lot of is white magic. He surprises himself by stating out loud a few comments, which brings doubt over himself.

- *Dam stupid evolution. All these crazy witchcrafts have mad me crazy. It's Simeon who is right. A job, a family, a little farm, kids to fill the yard and...*

John turns towards his cupboards.

- *...and a friend to confide in.*

John opens the cupboard and takes out his old bottle of vodka.

- *Hello Pierre.... I almost forgot about you.*

He takes his bottle, heads for his bed and lets himself fall on it like a child.

John cries all the tears of his being and finally does what resembles a prayer.

- *Mary...please, help me. Save me or save your son but one of the two is losing himself...*

Exhausted, John falls asleep on these words without taking any alcohol.

The horror starts up once again. John finds himself in the exact same dream, at the same place, in the same situation. He appears aware that he is dreaming and aware that he is there for the second time.

At the bottom of the mountain John takes control and climbs to the top without any difficulties.

Once at the top, he faces the macabre man and addresses him.

- *You will not win this time. Exclaims John.*

The horrible man gets up and attempts to grab John but he barely escapes him.

At this moment Kevin intervenes.

- *Let us play dad. You have no right.*
- *I have the right. I'm taking it. Replies John.*

John then grabs the king form the game board and places it in one of his pockets. The black man stands erected and gets angry with John.

- *You cannot remove a piece from the game. It's forbidden.*
- *Of course I can, see how easy it is you poor idiot.*

Then John runs away down the opposite side of the mountain.

The man chases him; John begins floating and lets the piece fall into space. Then he flies higher and higher. He reaches such a height that he can no longer see his pursuer.

During that time, since the game had lost its goal, Kevin leaves the scene and slowly climbs down the mountain. At the bottom he joins some friends who appear to know him well.

- *What happened?* Asks one of them.

As in any senseless dream Kevin casually answers;

- *Nothing. We did not get to finish. I lost my king but I did not lose the game.*

John then feels himself carried by this strong courant he already knew. He crosses the same dark tunnel at a very quick speed and feels himself falling into thin air, without nonetheless ever feeling uneasy.

John wakes up with a startle. He is, once again, sweating immensely and is breathing rapidly. He perfectly remembers the scene. He takes two minutes to recuperate and tells himself in a low voice.

- *It's over, we've actually won…*

He suddenly realizes that he did something he had never done before; he intervened in a dream to change the events of reality. Had he done well, had he broken the basic rules, will the billiard effect manifest itself in a good way? He only had to wait and se if all of this was related or not to concrete events.

John falls asleep again but keeps waking up, disturbed by the memory of this last dream. Come early morning John is woken by the phone.

- *Hello...*
- *Mr Chabot?* Asks the caller.
- *Yes, it's me.*
- *Mr John Chabot?*
- *That's correct. What's this about?* Asks John impatiently.
- *I am doctor Slodovnich from Trois-Rivieres.*
- *What's wrong.*
- *Nothing too serious Mr Chabot. We have a patient here by the name of Kevin Chabot.*
- *He says he is your son and requested we call you. He was transferred here from Sherbrooke last night.*
- *How is he?*
- *He's recuperating well. He regained conscious and asked that we call you. He wishes to see you as soon as possible.*
- *What happened?*
- *Their boat tipped over in one of the rapids. One of their friends was not so lucky. As for Kevin, he will be discharged in a couple of days. He requests to see you sir.*

John remains stunned and speechless. Then, disconcerted, concludes.

- *Tell him...I'll be right there.*

Arrived at the hospital, John slowly enters Kevin's room

Kevin is resting, connected to numerous medical equipment.

John approaches and gently sits on a chair near Kevin's bed.

Having felt the presence of someone in the room, Kevin painfully asks.

- *Is that you…dad?*
- *Yes son, it's me. Don't worry; the doctors say you will be just fine!*

Kevin cries silently. He attempts twice to speak but is choked up by his sorrow.

- *Don't worry son, everything will be all right now.*

Kevin painfully turns his head and looks at his father. John tenderly smiles at him.

- *I love you Kevin, I love you…*

Kevin takes all his strength and finally asks.

- *…how could you have known?*

Feeling cornered, John immediately admitted everything.

- *I was given the warning in a dream.*

Kevin begins crying even harder.

- *Forgive me dad…please forgive me.*

- *Come on, it's okay; you have to keep your strength. But tell me, what exactly happened. They told me that the boat capsized but even then...*

Kevin bursts out into tears and then explains.

- *Louis, the leader of our trip...he did not have his safety vest...he sank like a rock. I tried to go get him in the turbulence...I had him, I touched his hand but I don't know why, all of a sudden he slipped out of my hand, as though a strong courant dragged him deeper. After that, I couldn't do anything more...I wanted to continue.... then...I remembered what you told me...I began thinking of you...all of a sudden...then I quite trying...*

Kevin again bursts into tears believing he was responsible for his friend's death. Then he continues:

- *I let myself be carried by the courant...I must have hit a few rocks...*

Kevin lets out a few painful moans when the nurse shows up.

- *You must leave now Mr Chabot. He needs to rest. You can return in about three hours if you wish.*
- *Of course, I'll go now.*

John approaches Kevin and kisses his forehead. Kevin, still crying, manages to say:

- *I love you too dad...I love you too. Please forgive me.*

In an attempt to lighten the situation, John answers in a humoristic tone as he addresses the nurse.

- *I don't know what it is you're giving him...but double the dose*

John then leaves Kevin's room and takes the stairs leading to the exit. As he is about to leave the hospital, john runs into his personal doctor.

- *John, I'm quite happy to see you.*
- *Hello Doc. Have you heard...*
- *About your son...*
- *Yes, Kevin.*
- *I've heard about it. He was lucky.*

At wits end, John continues.

- *That's so true. He was lucky. But...I do not want to keep you; you must have your own patients to see.*
- *Actually, I wanted to speak with you John. Please come with me to my office.*

With a tired and heavy footing, John follows his doctor.
Once in his office, the doctor takes place in his chair and pulls out John's file from a pile holding about a dozen others.

- *We got the results of your last tests John.*
- *Tell me directly doctor before I tell you myself.*

The doctor takes a ceremonial attitude and confirms what John probably already knew.

- *It's regarding the pain in your back.*

- *Yeah, the pain in my back,* continues John in a casual manner.
- *It's a tumor John, your lungs are affected.*

John remains disinterested.
- *That's it doctor?*
- *But..we have effective treatments John…we can delay..*
- *My death?…No thanks, my road ends here. Anyway, I'm feeling trapped in this old body!*
- *There are tumors John, I first recommend chemotherapy…*
- *Thanks but it's not for me. I know of a much more efficient way but…someone is waiting for me up there.*

John rolls his hat between his hands and curiously shows a smile.

- *I've been waiting to see her for so long…*
- *But John…*
- *Forgive me doctor, I' don't have much time. I have things to do.*

John gets up, salutes the doctor and leaves the hospital.

Six months have gone by. John has definitely regained contact with his son Kevin.

On several occasions Kevin visited John. They often discussed the signification of dreams but John always only said very little about this and even tried to render it unimportant, knowing that Kevin is not yet ready for the entire truth.

Kevin was aware of his father's medical condition and wanted to take advantage of this time left to really get to know him.

He realized that behind this image that John kept of himself throughout all these years, there was a very wise man whom he now admires.

Meanwhile, John kept his knowledge on the spiritual world a secret.

Kevin did not try to know more, he was content in the fact that he was getting close to his father.

As for Simeon, he also multiplied is visits and frequently met with his nephew Kevin, with whom he had developed an affinity similar to that of which he had with John.

John also decided to inform Solenne of his situation and she agreed not to attempt intervening with his condition and his decision to leave.

- *I would really like to keep you John and I know that Leopold could help but I accept your choice and I know that you are now moving on to something different, something we will all, on day, be heading towards.*
- *I found the door Solenne, I finally found the door…*

On the day of John's funeral, Kevin said the eulogy which surprised everyone. The local people were stupefied by the profound declarations that he did in regard to his father.

Also, according to John's last wishes, at the end of the ceremony, a man, unknown to everyone there and who was dressed in white with also a white well trimmed beard was seen a distance away from the crowd. He was standing next to a luxurious white limousine and accompanied by Solenne. Nobody noticed their arrival.

The man then headed towards the group gathered in the cemetery. Everyone stopped talking, the priest interrupted his ritual, and all eyes were fixed on this strange and mysterious person. He made his way up to Kevin who had noticed him approaching and kept direct eye contact with him.

- *Mr Chabot?* Stated this man in a warm and friendly tone.
- *Yes.* Replied Kevin attempting to hold back his tears.
- *Your father requested I give you this.*

With a light smile of compassion on his face and as they were about to lower John's casket into the ground, he handed a very heavy suitcase to Kevin.

Kevin took the suitcase without any reaction and then the mysterious man left the scene. Kevin remained numb, suitcase in hand without realizing the rich heritage he had just received.

The priest resumed his ceremony and everyone then resumed their entire attention to the last moment of respects being paid to John.

Solenne had remained next to the limousine, observing the scene from afar. She sheds a few tears and speaks to herself.

• *See you soon John…you were always quicker than everyone…*

The priest's speech barely concluded and believing to have lacked in politeness, Kevin wanted to thank the mysterious man but when he looks up he was stunned and surprised to see that the man, Solenne and the limousine were nowhere to be found…

To be continued.

www.ingramcontent.com/pod-product-compliance
Lightning Source LLC
Chambersburg PA
CBHW061402280526
45784CB00001B/336